Q: Skills for Success 1

LISTENING AND SPEAKING

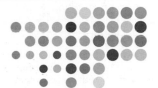

Jaimie Scanlon

SERIES CONSULTANTS

Marguerite Ann Snow

Lawrence J. Zwier

VOCABULARY CONSULTANT

Cheryl Boyd Zimmerman

OXFORD

UNIVERSITY PRESS

OXFORD
UNIVERSITY PRESS

198 Madison Avenue
New York, NY 10016 USA

Great Clarendon Street, Oxford OX2 6DP UK

Oxford University Press is a department of the University of Oxford.
It furthers the University's objective of excellence in research, scholarship,
and education by publishing worldwide in

Oxford New York

Auckland Cape Town Dar es Salaam Hong Kong Karachi
Kuala Lumpur Madrid Melbourne Mexico City Nairobi
New Delhi Shanghai Taipei Toronto

With offices in

Argentina Austria Brazil Chile Czech Republic France Greece
Guatemala Hungary Italy Japan Poland Portugal Singapore
South Korea Switzerland Thailand Turkey Ukraine Vietnam

OXFORD and OXFORD ENGLISH are registered trademarks of
Oxford University Press in certain countries.

General Manager, American ELT: Laura Pearson
Publisher: Stephanie Karras
Associate Publishing Manager: Sharon Sargent
Managing Editors: Martin Coleman, Mary Whittemore
Associate Development Editors: Rebecca Mostov, Keyana Shaw
Director, ADP: Susan Sanguily
Executive Design Manager: Maj-Britt Hagsted
Associate Design Manager: Michael Steinhofer
Electronic Production Manager: Julie Armstrong
Production Artist: Elissa Santos
Cover Design: Molly Scanlon
Image Manager: Trisha Masterson
Image Editors: Robin Fadool and Liaht Pashayan
Production Coordinator: Elizabeth Matsumoto

ISBN: 978-0-19-475610-5 Listening Speaking 1 Student Book Pack
ISBN: 978-0-19-475600-6 Listening Speaking 1 Student Book
ISBN: 978-0-19-475621-1 Q Online Practice Student Access Code Card

Printed in China

This book is printed on paper from certified and well-managed sources.

10 9 8 7 6

ACKNOWLEDGMENTS

*The publishers would like to thank the following for their kind permission to reproduce
photographs:* Cover John Giustina/Iconica/Getty Images; Sean Justice/Riser/
Getty Images; Kirsty Pargeter/iStockphoto; Leontura/iStockphoto; Illustrious/
iStockphoto; p. 2 Jeffrey Blackler/Alamy; p. 4 Andres Rodriguez/Alamy
(Elizabeth); p. 4 Westend61 GmbH/Alamy (Janek); p. 6 Visions of America,
LLC/Alamy (license plate); p. 6 OJO Images/Rex Features (business handshake);
p. 6 iStockphoto (friendly handshake); p. 10 Pictorial Press Ltd/Alamy (Ringo
Starr); p. 10 Kurt Krieger/Corbis UK Ltd. (Miley Cyrus); p. 10 Archives du 7eme
Art/Photo12.com (Bruce Lee); p. 10 Helen King/Corbis UK Ltd. (Hollywood);
p. 16 Blend Images/Alamy; p. 19 Kelly Redinger/Design Pics/Corbis UK Ltd.
(Sanjay); p. 19 Image Source/Alamy (Anita); p. 24 George Doyle/Stockbyte/
Getty Images; p. 26 Ian Sanderson/Getty Images (website designer);
p. 26 UpperCut Images/Alamy (server); p. 26 Barry Gnyp/UpperCut Images/
Getty Images (salesperson); p. 26 Corbis UK Ltd. (teacher); p. 28 Andersen
Ross/Blend Images/Corbis UK Ltd.; p. 31 GOGO Images/Superstock Ltd.;
p. 36 Image Source/Corbis UK Ltd.; p. 39 Inspirestock/Corbis UK Ltd.;
p. 44 ©Charles O. Cecil/The Image Works; p. 48 Dreamypix/Alamy;
p. 52 Directphoto.org/Alamy (bookstore); p. 52 Jgi/Blend Images/Corbis UK
Ltd. (flowers); p. 52 Amana Images inc./Alamy (business card); p. 52 Manfred
Rutz/Getty Images (bow); p. 54 Danita Delimont/Alamy; p. 59 Julie Armstrong
(all); p. 64 Jack Sullivan/Alamy; p. 64 TK (license plate); p. 68 No Ordinary Joe
(Joe Simpson); p. 68 Christian Kapteyn/Alamy (mountain); p. 70 Steven Vidler/
Eurasia Press/Corbis UK Ltd.; p. 71 Galina Barskaya/Alamy; p. 74 Tom Grill/
Corbis UK Ltd.; p. 75 Image Source/Alamy (studying); p. 75 ML Harris/Getty
Images (breakdown); p. 82 Kevin Arnold/Masterfile; p. 86 nagelestock.com/
Alamy (India); p. 86 Imagebroker/Alamy (Ecuador); p. 86 David Cherepuschak/
Alamy (Egypt); p. 86 Anna Yu/Alamy (bus); p. 89 Jon Arnold Images Ltd/
Alamy (Eiffel Tower); p. 89 Lonely Planet Images/Alamy (Angel Falls);
p. 89 Imagebroker/Alamy (Everest); p. 89 Philipus/Alamy (Burj Khalifa);
p. 91 Paul Springett 08/Alamy (Machu Picchu); p .91 Borderlands/Alamy
(teaching); p .91 Jim West/Alamy (painting); p .91 Bernd Tschakert/Alamy
(beach); p .91 Kiselev Andrey Valerevich/Shutterstock (backpack);
p96 Ian Buswell/Alamy; p .102 Evening Standard/Stringer/Hulton Archive/
Getty Images; p .104 Maskot/Alamy (computer); p .104 Masterfile UK Ltd.
(happy group); p .106 Blue Jean Images/Alamy (leap); p. 106 c.New Line/
Everett/Rex Features (shoe); p .106 Archives du 7eme Art/Photo12.com
(hands); p. 108 Ronald Grant Archive (Shanghai Noon); p. 108 c.Everett
Collection/Rex Features (Shinjuku Incident); p. 110 Amy Sussman/Getty
Images (comedian); p. 122 Corbis. All Rights Reserved; p. 126 Avatra Images/
Alamy; p. 127 Darama/Corbis UK Ltd.; p. 129 Blend Images/Alamy
(earphones); p. 129 DreamPictures/Blend Images/Getty Images (dancing);
p. 129 Matt Carr/Getty Images (guitar); p. 129 Paul Burns/Getty Images (mp3);
p. 129 Jeff Greenberg/Alamy (soccer); p. 137 Tim Pannell/Corbis UK Ltd.;
p. 140 Jetta Productions/Lifesize/Getty Images; p. 142 Nycretoucher/Getty
Images; p. 144 www.jupiterimages.com/Getty Images; p. 145 Markus
Moellenberg/Corbis UK Ltd.; p. 147 Wendy White/Alamy; p. 158 Journal-
Courier/Clayton Stalter/The Image Works; p. 162 Photodisc/Oxford University
Press; p. 164 Andres Rodriguez/Alamy; p. 165 PhotoAlto/Laurence Mouton/
Oxford University Press; p. 167 Zooid Pictures (books); p. 167 Tim Pannell/
Corbis UK Ltd. (DJ); p. 168 David R. Frazier Photolibrary, Inc./Alamy; p. 174
Catalin Petolea/Alamy; p. 178 Skip Brown/Nation Geographic/Getty Images;
p. 180 James Gerholdt/Peter Arnold Images/Photolibrary Group (snake);
p. 180 PhotoAlto/Alamy (elevator); p. 180 Radius Images/Alamy (speaker);
p. 180 Alex Benwell/Alamy (hights); p. 180 Barry Mason/Alamy (airplane);
p. 180 Shutterstock (lightning); p. 182 William Radcliffe/Science Faction/
Corbis UK Ltd.; p. 183 David Wall/Alamy; p. 185 Brownstock Inc./Oxford
University Press (fear); p. 185 Kiichiro Sato/AP Photo/Press Association Images
(platform); p. 186 James W. Porter/Corbis UK Ltd. (bed); p. 186 Pegaz/Alamy
(bridge); p. 193 Leonid Shanin - Animals/Alamy.

Illustrations by: p. 19 Bill Smith Group; p. 26 Barb Bastian; p. 40 Barb Bastian;
p. 46 Barb Bastian; p. 66 Jean Tuttle; p. 84 Barb Bastian; p. 89 Bill Smith
Group; p. 96 Bill Smith Group; p. 104 Bill Smith Group; p. 113 Mar Murube;
p. 114 Mar Murube; p. 116 Mar Murube; p. 124 Barb Bastian; p. 126 Jean
Tuttle; p. 142 Bill Smith Group; p. 154 Bill Smith Group; p. 160 Greg Paprocki;
p. 171 Barb Bastian; p. 180 Barb Bastian; p. 190 Jean Tuttle.

ACKNOWLEDGEMENTS

Author

Jaimie Scanlon holds an M.A. in TESOL and teaching French from the School for International Training, where she concentrated on language pedagogy, applied linguistics, and curriculum design. Over the past 15 years, she has taught English to learners of all ages, and has trained English teachers in Asia, Eastern Europe, and the U.S.

Series Consultants

Marguerite Ann Snow holds a Ph.D. in Applied Linguistics from UCLA. She is a Professor in the Charter College of Education at California State University, Los Angeles where she teaches in the TESOL M.A. program. She has published in *TESOL Quarterly*, *Applied Linguistics*, and *The Modern Language Journal*. She has been a Fulbright scholar in Hong Kong and Cyprus. In 2006, she received the President's Distinguished Professor award at Cal State LA. In addition to working closely with ESL and mainstream public school teachers in the U.S., she has trained EFL teachers in Algeria, Argentina, Brazil, Egypt, Japan, Morocco, Pakistan, Spain, and Turkey. Her main interests are integrated content and language instruction, English for Academic Purposes, and standards for English teaching and learning.

Lawrence J. Zwier holds an M.A. in TESL from the University of Minnesota. He is currently the Associate Director for Curriculum Development at the English Language Center at Michigan State University in East Lansing. He has taught ESL/EFL in the U.S., Saudi Arabia, Malaysia, Japan, and Singapore. He is a frequent TESOL conference presenter, and has published many ESL/EFL books in the areas of test-preparation, vocabulary, and reading, including *Inside Reading 2* for Oxford University Press.

Vocabulary Consultant

Cheryl Boyd Zimmerman is Associate Professor of TESOL at California State University, Fullerton. She specializes in second language vocabulary acquisition, an area in which she is widely published. She teaches graduate courses on second language acquisition, culture, vocabulary, and the fundamentals of TESOL, and is a frequent invited speaker on topics related to vocabulary teaching and learning. She is the author of *Word Knowledge: A Vocabulary Teacher's Handbook*, and Series Director of *Inside Reading*, both published by Oxford University Press.

REVIEWERS

We would like to acknowledge the advice of teachers from all over the world who participated in online reviews, focus groups, and editorial reviews. We relied heavily on teacher input throughout the extensive development process of the Q series, and many of the features in the series came directly from feedback we gathered from teachers in the classroom. We are grateful to all who helped.

UNITED STATES Marcarena Aguilar, North Harris College, TX; **Deborah Anholt**, Lewis and Clark College, OR; **Robert Anzelde**, Oakton Community College, IL; **Arlys Arnold**, University of Minnesota, MN; **Marcia Arthur**, Renton Technical College, WA; **Anne Bachmann**, Clackamas Community College, OR; **Ron Balsamo**, Santa Rosa Junior College, CA; **Lori Barkley**, Portland State University, OR; **Eileen Barlow**, SUNY Albany, NY; **Sue Bartch**, Cuyahoga Community College, OH; **Lora Bates**, Oakton High School, VA; **Nancy Baum**, University of Texas at Arlington, TX; **Linda Berendsen**, Oakton Community College, IL; **Jennifer Binckes Lee**, Howard Community College, MD; **Grace Bishop**, Houston Community College, TX; **Jean W. Bodman**, Union County College, NJ; **Virginia Bouchard**, George Mason University, VA; **Kimberley Briesch Sumner**, University of Southern California, CA; **Gabriela Cambiasso**, Harold Washington College, IL; **Jackie Campbell**, Capistrano Unified School District, CA; **Adele C. Camus**, George Mason University, VA; **Laura Chason**, Savannah College, GA; **Kerry Linder Catana**, Language Studies International, NY; **An Cheng**, Oklahoma State University, OK; **Carole Collins**, North Hampton Community College, PA; **Betty R. Compton**, Intercultural Communications College, HI; **Pamela Couch**, Boston University, MA; **Fernanda Crowe**, Intrax International Institute, CA; **Margo Czinski**, Washtenaw Community College, MI; **David Dahnke**, Lone Star College, TX; **Gillian M. Dale**, CA; **L. Dalgish**, Concordia College, MN; **Christopher Davis**, John Jay College, NY; **Sonia Delgadillo**, Sierra College, CA; **Marta O. Dmytrenko-Ahrabian**, Wayne State University, MI; **Javier Dominguez**, Central High School, SC; **Jo Ellen Downey-Greer**, Lansing Community College, MI; **Jennifer Duclos**, Boston University, MA; **Yvonne Duncan**, City College of San Francisco, CA; **Jennie Farnell**, University of Connecticut, CT; **Susan Fedors**, Howard Community College, MD; **Matthew Florence**, Intrax International Institute, CA; **Kathleen Flynn**, Glendale College, CA; **Eve Fonseca**, St. Louis Community College, MO; **Elizabeth Foss**, Washtenaw Community College, MI; **Duff C. Galda**, Pima Community College, AZ; **Christiane Galvani**, Houston Community College, TX; **Gretchen Gerber**, Howard Community College, MD; **Ray Gonzalez**, Montgomery College, MD; **Alyona Gorokhova**, Grossmont College, CA; **John Graney**, Santa Fe College, FL; **Kathleen Green**, Central High School, AZ; **Webb Hamilton**, De Anza College, San Jose City College, CA; **Janet Harclerode**, Santa Monica Community College, CA; **Sandra Hartmann**, Language and Culture Center, TX; **Kathy Haven**, Mission College, CA; **Adam Henricksen**, University of Maryland, MD; **Peter Hoffman**, LaGuardia Community College, NY; **Linda Holden**, College of Lake County, IL; **Jana Holt**, Lake Washington Technical College, WA; **Gail Ibele**, University of Wisconsin, WI; **Mandy Kama**, Georgetown University, Washington, DC; **Stephanie Kasuboski**, Cuyahoga Community College, OH; **Chigusa Katoku**, Mission College, CA; **Sandra Kawamura**, Sacramento City College, CA; **Gail Kellersberger**, University of Houston-Downtown, TX; **Jane Kelly**, Durham Technical Community College, NC; **Julie Park Kim**, George Mason University, VA; **Lisa Kovacs-Morgan** University of California, San Diego, CA; **Claudia Kupiec**, DePaul University, IL; **Renee La Rue**, Lone Star College-Montgomery, TX; **Janet Langon**, Glendale College, CA; **Lawrence Lawson**, Palomar College, CA; **Rachele Lawton**, The Community College of Baltimore County, MD; **Alice Lee**, Richland College, TX; **Cherie Lenz-Hackett**, University of Washington, WA; **Joy Leventhal**, Cuyahoga Community College, OH; **Candace Lynch-Thompson**, North Orange County Community College District, CA; **Thi Thi Ma**, City College of San Francisco, CA; **Denise Maduli-Williams**, City College of San Francisco, CA; **Eileen Mahoney**, Camelback High School, AZ; **Brigitte Maronde**, Harold Washington College, IL; **Keith Maurice**, University of Texas at Arlington, TX; **Nancy Mayer**, University of Missouri-St. Louis, MO; **Karen Merritt**, Glendale Union High School District, AZ; **Holly Milkowart**, Johnson County Community College, KS; **Eric Moyer**, Intrax International Institute, CA; **Gino Muzzatti**, Santa Rosa Junior College, CA; **William Nedrow**, Triton College, IL; **Eric Nelson**, University of Minnesota, MN; **Rhony Ory**, Ygnacio Valley High School, CA; **Paul Parent**, Montgomery College, MD; **Oscar Pedroso**, Miami Dade College, FL; **Robin Persiani**, Sierra College, CA; **Patricia Prenz-Belkin**, Hostos Community College, NY; **Jim Ranalli**, Iowa State University, IA; **Toni R. Randall**, Santa Monica College, CA; **Vidya Rangachari**, Mission College, CA; **Elizabeth Rasmussen**, Northern Virginia Community College, VA; **Lara Ravitch**, Truman College, IL; **Deborah Repasz**, San Jacinto College, TX; **Andrey Reznikov**, Black Hills State University, SD; **Alison Rice**, Hunter College, NY; **Jennifer Robles**, Ventura Unified School District, CA; **Priscilla Rocha**, Clark County School District, NV; **Dzidra Rodins**, DePaul University IL; **Maria Rodriguez**, Central High School, AZ; **Maria Ruiz**, Victor Valley College, CA; **Kimberly Russell**, Clark College, WA; **Irene Sakk**, Northwestern University, IL; **Shaeley Santiago**, Ames High School, IA; **Peg Sarosy**, San Francisco State University, CA; **Alice Savage**, North Harris College, TX; **Donna Schaeffer**, University of Washington, WA; **Carol Schinger**, Northern Virginia Community College, VA; **Robert Scott**, Kansas State University, KS; **Suell Scott**, Sheridan Technical Center, FL; **Shira Seaman**, Global English Academy, NY; **Richard Seltzer**, Glendale Community College, CA; **Kathy Sherak**, San Francisco State University, CA; **German Silva**, Miami Dade College, FL; **Andrea Spector**, Santa Monica Community College, CA; **Karen Stanely**, Central Piedmont Community College, NC; **Ayse Stromsdorfer**, Soldan I.S.H.S., MO; **Yilin Sun**, South Seattle Community College, WA; **Thomas Swietlik**, Intrax International Institute, IL; **Judith Tanka**, UCLA Extension–American Language Center, CA; **Priscilla Taylor**, University of Southern California, CA; **Ilene Teixeira**, Fairfax County Public Schools, VA; **Shirl H. Terrell**, Collin College, TX; **Marya Teutsch-Dwyer**, St. Cloud State University, MN; **Stephen Thergesen**, ELS Language Centers, CO; **Christine Tierney**, Houston Community College, TX; **Arlene Turini**, North Moore High School, NC; **Suzanne Van Der Valk**, Iowa State University, IA; **Nathan D. Vasarhely**, Ygnacio Valley High School, CA; **Naomi S. Verratti**, Howard Community College, MD; **Hollyahna Vettori**, Santa Rosa Junior College, CA; **Julie Vorholt**, Lewis & Clark College, OR; **Laura Walsh**, City College of San Francisco, CA; **Andrew J. Watson**, The English Bakery; **Donald Weasenforth**, Collin College, TX; **Juliane Widner**, Sheepshead Bay High School, NY; **Lynne Wilkins**, Mills College, CA; **Dolores "Lorrie" Winter**, California State University at Fullerton, CA; **Jody Yamamoto**, Kapi'olani Community College, HI; **Ellen L. Yaniv**, Boston University, MA; **Norman Yoshida**, Lewis & Clark College, OR; **Joanna Zadra**, American River College, CA; **Florence Zysman**, Santiago Canyon College, CA;

ASIA Rabiatu Abubakar, Eton Language Centre, Malaysia; **Wiwik Andreani**, Bina Nusantara University, Indonesia; **Mike Baker**, Kosei Junior High School, Japan; **Leonard Barrow**, Kanto Junior College, Japan; **Herman Bartelen**, Japan; **Siren Betty**, Fooyin University, Kaohsiung; **Thomas E. Bieri**, Nagoya College, Japan; **Natalie Brezden**, Global English House, Japan; **MK Brooks**, Mukogawa Women's University, Japan; **Truong Ngoc Buu**, The Youth Language School, Vietnam; **Charles Cabell**, Toyo University, Japan; **Fred Carruth**, Matsumoto University, Japan; **Frances Causer**, Seijo University, Japan; **Deborah Chang**, Wenzao Ursuline College of Languages, Kaohsiung; **David Chatham**, Ritsumeikan University, Japan; **Andrew Chih Hong Chen**, National Sun Yat-sen University, Kaohsiung; **Christina Chen**, Yu-Tsai Bilingual Elementary School, Taipei; **Jason Jeffree Cole**, Coto College, Japan; **Le Minh Cong**, Vungtau Tourism Vocational College, Vietnam; **Todd Cooper**, Toyama National College of Technology, Japan; **Marie Cosgrove**, Daito Bunka University, Japan; **Tony Cripps**, Ritsumeikan University, Japan; **Daniel Cussen**, Takushoku University, Japan; **Le Dan**, Ho Chi Minh City Electric Power College, Vietnam; **Simon Daykin**, Banghwa-dong Community Centre, South Korea; **Aimee Denham**, ILA, Vietnam; **Bryan Dickson**, David's English Center, Taipei; **Nathan Ducker**, Japan University, Japan; **Ian Duncan**, Simul International Corporate Training, Japan; **Nguyen Thi Kieu Dung**, Thang Long University, Vietnam; **Nguyen Thi Thuy Duong**, Vietnamese American Vocational Training College, Vietnam; **Wong Tuck Ee**, Raja Tun Azlan Science Secondary School, Malaysia; **Emilia Effendy**, International Islamic University Malaysia, Malaysia; **Robert Eva**, Kaisei Girls High School, Japan; **Jim George**, Luna International Language School, Japan; **Jurgen Germeys**, Silk Road Language Center, South Korea; **Wong Ai Gnoh**, SMJK Chung Hwa Confucian, Malaysia; **Peter Goosselink**, Hokkai High School,

Japan; **Wendy M. Gough**, St. Mary College/Nunoike Gaigo Senmon Gakko, Japan; **Tim Grose**, Sapporo Gakuin University, Japan; **Pham Thu Ha**, Le Van Tam Primary School, Vietnam; **Ann-Marie Hadzima**, Taipei; **Troy Hammond**, Tokyo Gakugei University International Secondary School, Japan; **Robiatul 'Adawiah Binti Hamzah**, SMK Putrajaya Precinct 8(1), Malaysia; **Tran Thi Thuy Hang**, Ho Chi Minh City Banking University, Vietnam; **To Thi Hong Hanh**, CEFALT, Vietnam; **Janis Hearn**, Hongik University, South Korea; **David Hindman**, Sejong University, South Korea; **Nahn Cam Hoa**, Ho Chi Minh City University of Technology, Vietnam; **Jana Holt**, Korea University, South Korea; **Jason Hollowell**, Nihon University, Japan; **F. N. (Zoe) Hsu**, National Tainan University, Yong Kang; **Wenhua Hsu**, I-Shou University, Kaohsiung; **Luu Nguyen Quoc Hung,** Cantho University, Vietnam ; **Cecile Hwang**, Changwon National University, South Korea; **Ainol Haryati Ibrahim**, Universiti Malaysia Pahang, Malaysia; **Robert Jeens**, Yonsei University, South Korea; **Linda M. Joyce**, Kyushu Sangyo University, Japan; **Dr. Nisai Kaewsanchai**, English Square Kanchanaburi, Thailand; **Aniza Kamarulzaman**, Sabah Science Secondary School, Malaysia; **Ikuko Kashiwabara**, Osaka Electro-Communication University, Japan; **Gurmit Kaur**, INTI College, Malaysia; **Nick Keane**, Japan; **Ward Ketcheson,** Aomori University, Japan; **Montchatry Ketmuni**, Rajamangala University of Technology, Thailand; **Dinh Viet Khanh**, Vietnam; **Seonok Kim**, Kangsu Jongro Language School, South Korea; **Kelly P. Kimura**, Soka University, Japan; **Stan Kirk**, Konan University, Japan; **Donald Knight**, Nan Hua/Fu Li Junior High Schools, Hsinchu; **Kari J. Kostiainen**, Nagoya City University, Japan; **Pattri Kuanpulpol**, Silpakorn University, Thailand; **Ha Thi Lan**, Thai Binh Teacher Training College, Vietnam; **Eric Edwin Larson**, Miyazaki Prefectural Nursing University, Japan; **Richard S. Lavin**, Prefectural University of Kumamoto, Japan; **Shirley Leane**, Chugoku Junior College, Japan; **Tae Lee**, Yonsei University, South Korea; **Lys Yongsoon Lee**, Reading Town Geumcheon, South Korea; **Mallory Leece**, Sun Moon University, South Korea, **Dang Hong Lien**, Tan Lam Upper Secondary School, Vietnam; **Huang Li-Han**, Rebecca Education Institute, Taipei; **Sovannarith Lim**, Royal University of Phnom Penh, Cambodia; **Ginger Lin**, National Kaohsiung Hospitality College, Kaohsiung; **Noel Lineker**, New Zealand/Japan; **Tran Dang Khanh Linh**, Nha Trang Teachers' Training College, Vietnam; **Daphne Liu**, Buliton English School, Taipei; **S. F. Josephine Liu**, Tien Mu Elementary School, Taipei ; **Caroline Luo**, Tunghai University, Taichung; **Jeng-Jia Luo**, Tunghai University, Taichung; **Laura MacGregor**, Gakushuin University, Japan; **Amir Madani**, Visutharangsi School, Thailand; **Elena Maeda**, Sacred Heart Professional Training College, Japan; **Vu Thi Thanh Mai**, Hoang Gia Education Center, Vietnam; **Kimura Masakazu**, Kato Gakuen Gyoshu High School, Japan; **Susumu Matsuhashi**, Net Link English School, Japan; **James McCrostie**, Daito Bunka University, Japan; **Joel McKee**, Inha University, South Korea; **Colin McKenzie**, Wachirawit Primary School, Thailand; **William K. Moore**, Hiroshima Kokusai Gakuin University, Japan; **Hudson Murrell**, Baiko Gakuin University, Japan; **Frances Namba**, Senri International School of Kwansei Gakuin, Japan; **Keiichi Narita**, Niigata University, Japan; **Kim Chung Nguyen**, Ho Chi Minh University of Industry, Vietnam; **Do Thi Thanh Nhan**, Hanoi University, Vietnam; **Dale Kazuo Nishi**, Aoyama English Conversation School, Japan; **Louise Ohashi**, Shukutoku University, Japan; **Virginia Peng**, Ritsumeikan University, Japan; **Suangkanok Piboonthamnont**, Rajamangala University of Technology, Thailand; **Simon Pitcher**, Business English Teaching Services, Japan; **John C. Probert**, New Education Worldwide, Thailand; **Do Thi Hoa Quyen**, Ton Duc Thang University, Vietnam; **John P. Racine**, Dokkyo University, Japan; **Kevin Ramsden**, Kyoto University of Foreign Studies, Japan; **Luis Rappaport**, Cung Thieu Nha Ha Noi, Vietnam; **Lisa Reshad**, Konan Daigaku Hyogo, Japan; **Peter Riley**, Taisho University, Japan; **Thomas N. Robb**, Kyoto Sangyo University, Japan; **Maria Feti Rosyani**, Universitas Kristen Indonesia, Indonesia; **Greg Rouault**, Konan University, Japan; **Chris Ruddenklau**, Kindai University, Japan; **Hans-Gustav Schwartz**, Thailand; **Mary-Jane Scott**, Soongsil University, South Korea; **Jenay Seymour**, Hongik University, South Korea; **James Sherlock**, A.P.W. Angthong, Thailand; **Yuko Shimizu**, Ritsumeikan University, Japan; **Suzila Mohd Shukor**, Universiti Sains Malaysia, Malaysia; **Stephen E. Smith**, Mahidol University, Thailand; **Mi-young Song**, Kyungwon University, South Korea; **Jason Stewart**, Taejon International Language School, South Korea; **Brian A. Stokes**, Korea University, South Korea; **Mulder Su**, Shih-Chien University, Kaohsiung;

Yoomi Suh, English Plus, South Korea; **Yun-Fang Sun**, Wenzao Ursuline College of Languages, Kaohsiung; **Richard Swingle**, Kansai Gaidai University, Japan; **Tran Hoang Tan**, School of International Training, Vietnam; **Takako Tanaka**, Doshisha University, Japan; **Jeffrey Taschner**, American University Alumni Language Center, Thailand ; **Michael Taylor**, International Pioneers School, Thailand; **Tran Duong The**, Sao Mai Language Center, Vietnam; **Tran Dinh Tho**, Duc Tri Secondary School, Vietnam; **Huynh Thi Anh Thu**, Nhatrang College of Culture Arts and Tourism, Vietnam; **Peter Timmins**, Peter's English School, Japan; **Fumie Togano**, Hosei Daini High School, Japan; **F. Sigmund Topor**, Keio University Language School, Japan; **Yen-Cheng Tseng**, Chang-Jung Christian University, Tainan; **Hajime Uematsu**, Hirosaki University, Japan; **Rachel Um**, Mok-dong Oedae English School, South Korea; **David Underhill**, EEExpress, Japan; **Siriluck Usaha**, Sripatum University, Thailand; **Tyas Budi Utami**, Indonesia; **Nguyen Thi Van**, Far East International School, Vietnam; **Stephan Van Eycken**, Kosei Gakuen Girls High School, Japan; **Zisa Velasquez**, Taihu International School/Semarang International School, China/Indonesia; **Jeffery Walter**, Sangji University, South Korea; **Bill White**, Kinki University, Japan; **Yohanes De Deo Widyastoko**, Xaverius Senior High School, Indonesia; **Greg Chung-Hsien Wu**, Providence University, Taichung; **Hui-Lien Yeh**, Chai Nan University of Pharmacy and Science, Tainan; **Sittiporn Yodnil**, Huachiew Chalermprakiet University, Thailand; **Shamshul Helmy Zambahari**, Universiti Teknologi Malaysia, Malaysia; **Ming-Yuli**, Chang Jung Christian University, Tainan; **Aimin Fadhlee bin Mahmud Zuhodi**, Kuala Terengganu Science School, Malaysia;

TURKEY **Gül Akkoç**, Boğaziçi University; **Seval Akmeşe**, Haliç University; **Deniz Balım**, Haliç University; **Robert Ledbury**, Izmir University of Economics; **Oya Özağaç**, Boğaziçi University;

THE MIDDLE EAST **Amina Saif Mohammed Al Hashamia**, Nizwa College of Applied Sciences, Oman; **Sharon Ruth Devaneson**, Ibri College of Technology, Oman; **Hanaa El-Deeb**, Canadian International College, Egypt; **Brian Gay**, Sultan Qaboos University, Oman; **Gail Al-Hafidh**, Sharjah Higher Colleges of Technology, U.A.E.; **Jonathan Hastings**, American Language Center, Jordan; **Sian Khoury**, Fujairah Women's College (HCT), U.A.E.; **Jessica March**, American University of Sharjah, U.A.E.; **Neil McBeath**, Sultan Qaboos University, Oman;

LATIN AMERICA **Aldana Aguirre**, Argentina; **Claudia Almeida**, Coordenação de Idiomas, Brazil; **Cláudia Arias**, Brazil; **María de los Angeles Barba**, FES Acatlan UNAM, Mexico; **Lilia Barrios**, Universidad Autónoma de Tamaulipas, Mexico; **Adán Beristain**, UAEM, Mexico; **Ricardo Böck**, Manoel Ribas, Brazil; **Edson Braga**, CNA, Brazil; **Marli Buttelli**, Mater et Magistra, Brazil; **Alessandra Campos**, Inova Centro de Linguas, Brazil; **Priscila Catta Preta Ribeiro**, Brazil; **Gustavo Cestari**, Access International School, Brazil; **Walter D'Alessandro**, Virginia Language Center, Brazil; **Lilian De Gennaro**, Argentina; **Mônica De Stefani**, Quality Centro de Idiomas, Brazil; **Julio Alejandro Flores**, BUAP, Mexico; **Mirian Freire**, CNA Vila Guilherme, Brazil; **Francisco Garcia**, Colegio Lestonnac de San Angel, Mexico; **Miriam Giovanardi**, Brazil; **Darlene Gonzalez Miy**, ITESM CCV, Mexico; **Maria Laura Grimaldi**, Argentina; **Luz Dary Guzmán**, IMPAHU, Colombia; **Carmen Koppe**, Brazil; **Monica Krutzler**, Brazil; **Marcus Murilo Lacerda**, Seven Idiomas, Brazil; **Nancy Lake**, CEL-LEP, Brazil; **Cris Lazzerini**, Brazil; **Sandra Luna**, Argentina; **Ricardo Luvisan**, Brazil; **Jorge Murilo Menezes**, ACBEU, Brazil; **Monica Navarro**, Instituto Cultural A. C., Mexico; **Joacyr Oliveira**, Faculdades Metropolitanas Unidas and Summit School for Teachers, Brazil; **Ayrton Cesar Oliveira de Araujo**, E&A English Classes, Brazil; **Ana Laura Oriente**, Seven Idiomas, Brazil; **Adelia Peña Clavel**, CELE UNAM, Mexico; **Beatriz Pereira**, Summit School, Brazil; **Miguel Perez**, Instituto Cultural Mexico; **Cristiane Perone**, Associação Cultura Inglesa, Brazil; **Pamela Claudia Pogré**, Colegio Integral Caballito / Universidade de Flores, Argentina; **Dalva Prates**, Brazil; **Marianne Rampaso**, Iowa Idiomas, Brazil; **Daniela Rutolo**, Instituto Superior Cultural Británico, Argentina; **Maione Sampaio**, Maione Carrijo Consultoria em Inglês Ltda, Brazil; **Elaine Santesso**, TS Escola de Idiomas, Brazil; **Camila Francisco Santos**, UNS Idiomas, Brazil; **Lucia Silva**, Cooplem Idiomas, Brazil; **Maria Adela Sorzio**, Instituto Superior Santa Cecilia, Argentina; **Elcio Souza**, Unibero, Brazil; **Willie Thomas**, Rainbw Idiomas, Brazil; **Sandra Villegas**, Instituto Humberto de Paolis, Argentina; **John Whelan**, La Universidad Nacional Autonoma de Mexico, Mexico

WELCOME TO Q:Skills for Success

Q: Skills for Success is a six-level series with two strands, *Reading and Writing* and *Listening and Speaking*.

READING AND WRITING

LISTENING AND SPEAKING

WITH Q ONLINE PRACTICE

STUDENT AND TEACHER INFORMED

Q: Skills for Success is the result of an extensive development process involving thousands of teachers and hundreds of students around the world. Their views and opinions helped shape the content of the series. *Q* is grounded in teaching theory as well as real-world classroom practice, making it the most learner-centered series available.

CONTENTS

Quick Guide viii

Scope and Sequence xiv

Unit 1 **Q: Do you like your name?** 2
    Listening 1: Given Names and Nicknames
    Listening 2: Stage Names
    Q Online Practice Listening: Naming Foods

Unit 2 **Q: How can you find a good job?** 24
    Listening 1: Looking for a Job
    Listening 2: The Right Person for the Right Job
    Q Online Practice Listening: What Makes a Good Manager?

Unit 3 **Q: Why do we study other cultures?** 44
    Listening 1: International Advertising
    Listening 2: Culture Problems
    Q Online Practice Listening: My Grandmother

Unit 4 **Q: What makes a happy ending?** 64
    Listening 1: A Bad Situation with a Happy Ending
    Listening 2: Make Your Own Happy Ending
    Q Online Practice Listening: My Happy Ending

Unit 5 **Q: What is the best vacation?** 82
    Listening 1: Places in Danger
    Listening 2: A Helpful Vacation
    Q Online Practice Listening: The Peace Boat

Unit 6 **Q: Who makes you laugh?** 102
    Listening 1: Jackie Chan—Action-Comedy Hero
    Listening 2: Can Anyone Be Funny?
    Q Online Practice Listening: Comedy Movie Reviews

Unit 7 **Q: Why is music important to you?** 122
    Listening 1: Mind, Body, and Music
    Listening 2: Music in Our Lives
    Q Online Practice Listening: Umm Kalthoum

Unit 8 **Q: When is honesty important?** 140
    Listening 1: Dishonesty in Schools
    Listening 2: What's the Right Thing to Do?
    Q Online Practice Listening: Is Downloading Dishonest?

Unit 9 **Q: Is it ever too late to change?** 158
    Listening 1: Attitudes about Change
    Listening 2: Tips From a Life Coach
    Q Online Practice Listening: Changing Careers

Unit 10 **Q: When is it good to be afraid?** 178
    Listening 1: The Science of Fear
    Listening 2: What Are You Afraid of?
    Q Online Practice Listening: Conquering Fear

Audioscript 196

Q connects critical thinking, language skills, and learning outcomes.

LANGUAGE SKILLS

Explicit skills instruction enables students to meet their academic and professional goals.

LEARNING OUTCOMES

Clearly identified **learning outcomes** focus students on the goal of their instruction.

UNIT 6

Laughter

LISTENING	listening for specific information
VOCABULARY	synonyms
GRAMMAR	simple present for informal narratives
PRONUNCIATION	simple present third-person *-s/-es*
SPEAKING	using eye contact, pause, and tone of voice

LEARNING OUTCOME

Use appropriate eye contact, tone of voice, and pauses to tell a funny story or a joke to your classmates.

Unit QUESTION

Who makes you laugh?

PREVIEW THE UNIT

A Discuss these questions with your classmates.

What funny movie or TV show do you like?

Do you tell jokes or make other people laugh?

Look at the photo. Do you think it is funny? Why or why not?

B Discuss the Unit Question above with your classmates.

 Listen to *The Q Classroom*, Track 16 on CD 2, to hear other answers.

102 UNIT 6

103

CRITICAL THINKING

Thought-provoking **unit questions** engage students with the topic and provide a **critical thinking framework** for the unit.

> " Having the learning outcome is important because it gives students and teachers a clear idea of what the point of each task/activity in the unit is. "
> *Lawrence Lawson, Palomar College, California*

PREVIEW LISTENING 1

Jackie Chan—Action-Comedy Hero

You are going to listen to a radio program about Jackie Chan, a popular
action-comedy film star. Look at the photos. Why do you think people
will say Jackie Chan is funny? Give two reasons.

Q WHAT DO YOU THINK?

A. Discuss the questions in a group.

1. Do you agree that anyone can be funny? Why or why not?

2. Do you think Tate's advice is good? What other advice would you give
   to help people be funny?

3. What are favorite funny topics in your culture?

**B. Think about both Listening 1 and Listening 2 as you discuss
the questions.**

1. How is the humor in a comedy film different than in a live theater? How
   are they the same?

Explicit skills instruction prepares students for academic success.

LANGUAGE SKILLS

Explicit instruction and practice in listening, speaking, grammar, pronunciation, and vocabulary skills **help students achieve language proficiency.**

Q WHAT DO YOU THINK?

Discuss the questions in a group.

1. Why do people think Jackie Chan is funny? Do you think this type of sense of humor is funny?

2. Do you like *Kung Fu* or other similar movies? Why or why not?

3. Who are famous comedy stars from your country? Why do you think they are popular?

| Listening Skill | Listening for specific information |  |

Listening for specific information means listening for the important details you need. We listen for specific information especially when we listen to news or weather reports, transportation schedules, and instructions. Specific information includes details such as:

- names of people or places
- numbers, dates, or times (See Unit 5 Listening Skill, pages 87–88.)
- events

CD 2
Track 19

A. Read the information below. Then listen to Listening 1 again and write the missing information.

1. Jackie Chan's birth date: _____.

2. When he moved to Hollywood: _____.

3. What Americans thought of Chan in *Rush Hour*: _____.

4. Three reasons why he is funny:

 a. He smiles and _____.

 b. He's so _____.

 c. Fans love watching _____.

| Listening and Speaking **107**

LEARNING OUTCOMES

Practice activities allow students to **master the skills** before they are evaluated at the end of the unit.

| Speaking Skill | Using eye contact, pause, and tone of voice | |

When you tell a story or a joke, there are different ways to make it more interesting.

- **Make eye contact with the listener(s).** This will help you connect with your audience and keep them interested.
- **Use your voice to express different feelings.** This helps the listener understand the feelings of the people in the story.
- **Pause—stop speaking for a moment—**before you say the punch line (the end of a story or joke). This can help to make the ending a surprise.

CD 2
Track 25

Listen to the example.

...The man touches the rabbit, and the rabbit bites him.
"Ouch!" He says, "You said your rabbit doesn't bite!"
surprised/angry tone of voice

The shopkeeper replies, "That isn't my rabbit!"
↑
pause

CD 2
Track 26

A. Listen to the excerpts from the jokes. Underline the places where the speaker uses tone of voice. Draw an arrow (↑) where the speaker pauses.

1. One day, I'm at home. I turn on the TV and sit down on the sofa. My wife asks, "What are you doing?" I say, "Nothing." She says, "You did that yesterday." So I answer, "Yeah, I know. I wasn't finished."

2. The woman answers, "I hurt everywhere. It hurts when I touch my head. It hurts when I touch my leg, and it hurts when I touch my arm." The doctor thinks for a moment. Then he says, "I know what's wrong... Your finger is broken!"

B. Work with a partner. Read the excerpts from Activity A aloud. Practice making eye contact, using tone of voice, and pausing.

| Listening and Speaking **117**

 The tasks are simple, accessible, user-friendly, and very useful.
Jessica March, American University of Sharjah, U.A.E.

Vocabulary Skill	Synonyms	web⁺

Synonyms are words that have almost the same or a similar meaning. The dictionary often gives synonyms in the definition of a word. In the examples, a synonym is given for *funny* while for *movie* only a definition is provided.

fun·ny 🔑 /ˈfʌni/ *adjective* (fun·ni·er, fun·ni·est)
1 making you laugh or smile: *a funny story* • *He's so funny!* ⊃ **SYNONYM amusing**
2 strange or surprising: *There's a funny smell in this room.*

mov·ie 🔑 /ˈmuvi/ *noun*
1 [*count*] a story shown in moving pictures that you see in theaters or on television: *Would you like to see a movie?*

You can build your vocabulary by learning synonyms for words you already know. Learning synonyms will help you understand more when you listen.

All dictionary entries are taken from the *Oxford American Dictionary for learners of English*.

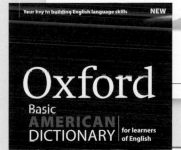

All dictionary entries are taken from the *Oxford Basic American Dictionary for learners of English*.

The **Oxford American Dictionary for learners of English** was designed with English learners in mind, and provides extra learning tools for pronunciation, verb types, basic grammar structures, and more.

The Oxford 2000 Keywords 🔑
The Oxford 2000 Keywords encompasses the 2000 most important words to learn in English. It is based on a comprehensive analysis of the Oxford English Corpus, a two billion word collection of English text, and on extensive research with both language and pedagogical experts.

The Academic Word List ⬛AWL⬛
The Academic Word List was created by Averil Coxhead and contains **570 words that are commonly used in academic English**, such as in textbooks or articles across a wide range of academic subject areas. These words are a great place to start if you are studying English for academic purposes.

Clear learning outcomes focus students on the goals of instruction.

Unit Assignment **Tell a joke or a funny story**

 In this assignment, you are going to tell a funny story or joke to a group (or to the class). Use some of the tips from this unit to add interest and humor. Think about the question, "Who makes you laugh?" and refer to the Self-Assessment checklist on page 120 as you prepare to tell your joke or story.

For alternative unit assignments, see the *Q: Skills for Success Teacher's Handbook.*

CONSIDER THE IDEAS

Complete the tasks.

1. Read the joke and try to guess the punch line (the last line). Then listen to check your answer.

   A tourist visits Sydney, Australia. He wants to go to the beach. But he doesn't know how to get there. He sees a policeman. He waves to the policeman and says, "Excuse me! Can you help me?"

   The policeman comes over and says, "Yes, sir. How can I help you?"

   The tourist says, "Can you tell me the fastest way to get to the beach?"

Check (✓) the skills you learned. If you need more work on a skill, refer to the page(s) in parentheses.

LISTENING	I can listen for specific information. (p. 107)
VOCABULARY	I can recognize and use synonyms. (p. 111)
GRAMMAR	I can recognize and use the simple present for informal narratives. (p. 113)
PRONUNCIATION	I can recognize and use the simple present third-person *-s/-es*. (p. 115)
SPEAKING	I can use eye contact, pause, and tone of voice. (p. 117)
LEARNING OUTCOME	I can use appropriate eye contact, tone of voice, and pauses to tell a funny story or a joke to my classmates.

 Students can check their learning . . . and they can focus on the essential points when they study.

Suh Yoomi, Seoul, South Korea

Q Online Practice

For the student

- **Easy-to-use:** a simple interface allows students to focus on enhancing their speaking and listening skills, not learning a new software program
- **Flexible:** for use anywhere there's an Internet connection
- **Access code card:** a *Q Online Practice* access code is included with this book—use the access code to register for *Q Online Practice* at www.Qonlinepractice.com

For the teacher

- **Simple yet powerful:** automatically grades student exercises and tracks progress
- **Straightforward:** online management system to review, print, or export the reports they need
- **Flexible:** for use in the classroom or easily assigned as homework
- **Access code card:** contact your sales rep for your *Q Online Practice* teacher's access code

Teacher Resources

For additional resources visit the
Q: Skills for Success companion website at
www.oup.com/elt/teacher/Qskillsforsuccess

Q Teacher's Handbook gives strategic support through:
- specific teaching notes for each activity
- ideas for ensuring student participation
- multilevel strategies and expansion activities
- the answer key
- special sections on 21st Century Skills and critical thinking
- a *Testing Program CD-ROM* with a customizable test for each unit

Q Class Audio includes:
- listening texts
- pronunciation presentations and exercises
- *The Q Classroom*

> " It's an interesting, engaging series which provides plenty of materials that are easy to use in class, as well as instructionally promising. "
> *Donald Weasenforth, Collin College, Texas*

UNIT	LISTENING	SPEAKING	VOCABULARY
1 Names **Q Do you like your name?** **LISTENING 1: Given Names and Nicknames** A Group Discussion (Cultural Anthropology) **LISTENING 2: Stage Names** A Radio Talk-Show (Linguistics)	• Predict content • Listen for main ideas • Listen for details • Listen for examples to better understand main ideas • Listen for reasons in order to understand a partner's background • Listen for sentence intonation to understand types of questions	• Take notes to prepare for a presentation or group discussion • Ask follow-up questions to keep a conversation going • Talk about reasons in order to explain your actions • Interview people to find out about their backgrounds	• Assess your prior knowledge of vocabulary • Prefixes that mean *not*
2 Work **Q How can you find a good job?** **LISTENING 1: Looking for a Job** An Online Job Search (Management) **LISTENING 2: The Right Person for the Job** A Job Interview (Human Resources)	• Predict content • Listen for main ideas • Listen for details • Understand key words and phrases to identify a topic • Listen for specific vocabulary items in context to figure out their meanings • Understand personal questions to describe yourself to an interviewer • Recognize word boundaries in a stream of speech to identify important vocabulary	• Take notes to prepare for a presentation or group discussion • Discuss qualities of applicants to determine the best for a job • Ask for repetition and clarification to make sure you understand • Role-play an interview to practice conversational skills and vocabulary use	• Assess your prior knowledge of vocabulary • Use a dictionary to distinguish between words with similar meanings
3 Long Distance **Q Why do we study other cultures?** **LISTENING 1: International Advertising** A Business Class Lecture (Anthropology) **LISTENING 2: Cultural Problems** Three Different Perspectives (Advertising)	• Predict content • Listen for main ideas • Listen for details • Practice listening to a lecture to identify problems mentioned by the speaker • Organize notes to show the structure of a passage • Identify individual words within sentences to understand key concepts • Listen for directions to understand what *should/should not* be done	• Take notes to prepare for a presentation or group discussion • Work from notes to give a well-organized presentation • Maintain eye contact to keep a conversation partner engaged • Describe a personal experience to illustrate your cultural background	• Assess your prior knowledge of vocabulary • Use context to guess meanings of unfamiliar words

GRAMMAR	PRONUNCIATION	CRITICAL THINKING	UNIT OUTCOME
• Simple present statements and questions	• Intonation in *yes/no* and information questions	• Assess your prior knowledge of content • Relate personal experiences to listening topics • Integrate information from multiple sources • Reflect on what you have learned in the unit • Speculate about choices you might make • Recall personal histories • Appreciate formal and informal speaking situations	• Interview a classmate and introduce him/her to the class using the simple present tense
• Simple past • Regular and irregular verbs	• Past tense *-ed* endings	• Assess your prior knowledge of content • Relate personal experiences to listening topics • Integrate information from multiple sources • Reflect on what you have learned in the unit • Identify qualifications necessary for a task • Examine personal attributes and abilities • Assess personal preferences	• Write interview questions and role-play a job interview
• *Should/shouldn't* • *It's* + adjective + infinitive	• Reduced vowels (represented by the schwa /ə/ sound)	• Assess your prior knowledge of content • Relate personal experiences to listening topics • Integrate information from multiple sources • Reflect on what you have learned in the unit • Infer ideas from pictures • Compare and contrast cultures • Anticipate problems and suggest solutions	• Give a presentation about customs in a culture you know well

UNIT	LISTENING	SPEAKING	VOCABULARY
4 **Positive Thinking** **Q** **What makes a happy ending?** **LISTENING 1: A Bad Situation with a Happy Ending** A True Story (Psychology) **LISTENING 2: Make Your Own Happy Ending** A Radio Interview (Anthropology)	• Predict content • Listen for main ideas • Listen for details • Listen for reasons so you can better understand other people's beliefs • Apply questions like *who*, *what*, *when*, etc., to understand the basics of a story • Listen for syllable stress to recognize words in speech	• Take notes to prepare for a presentation or group discussion • Use expressions of interest to keep a conversation going • Organize information for a discussion • Use reasons to explain personal beliefs	• Assess your prior knowledge of vocabulary • Use a dictionary to find parts of speech
5 **Vacation Time** **Q** **What is the best kind of vacation?** **LISTENING 1: Places In Danger** A Podcast of a Travel Program (Ecology) **LISTENING 2: A Helpful Vacation** A Presentation about Volunteer Jobs (Hospitality and Tourism)	• Predict content • Listen for main ideas • Listen for details • Recognize numbers and dates to understand specific details • Take notes to identify support for main ideas • Recognize reduced forms to understand informal speech • Sort facts into categories to see content relationships	• Take notes to prepare for a presentation or group discussion • Use structure signals to introduce topics in a presentation • Ask follow-up questions to keep a conversation going • Express reasons to justify personal choices	• Assess your prior knowledge of vocabulary • Use the suffixes *-ful* and *-ing* to form adjectives
6 **Laughter** **Q** **Who makes you laugh?** **LISTENING 1: Jackie Chan— Action-Comedy Hero** A Radio Program (Film Study) **LISTENING 2: Can Anyone Be Funny?** A TV Interview (Psychology)	• Predict content • Listen for main ideas • Listen for details • Listen for exact words or phrases to improve your word recognition • Recognize sequence words to understand a flow of ideas • Listen for names and numbers to understand details in a passage • Recognize jokes to understand a speaker's intent	• Take notes to prepare for a presentation or group discussion • Use eye contact, pauses, and tone of voice to relate well to an audience • Include jokes or funny stories to make a presentation more interesting • Use narrative present verbs to create an informal tone	• Assess your prior knowledge of vocabulary • Use synonyms to give variety to speech
7 **Music** **Q** **Why is music important to you?** **LISTENING 1: Mind, Body, and Music** A University Lecture (Physiology) **LISTENING 2: Music in Our Lives** A Discussion (Psychology)	• Predict content • Listen for main ideas • Listen for details • Listen for enumeration signals to understand the structure of a passage • Understand answers in an interview to learn about someone's tastes and preferences • Listen for opinions to understand someone's attitudes and tastes	• Take notes to prepare for a presentation or group discussion • Ask follow-up questions to keep a conversation going • Converse politely, express your tastes and preferences, and ask about someone else's • Talk about musical tastes • Conduct an interview to practice asking questions about choice	• Assess your prior knowledge of vocabulary • Use the dictionary to find the correct definition of a word with several meanings

GRAMMAR	PRONUNCIATION	CRITICAL THINKING	UNIT OUTCOME
• *Because* and *so*	• Word stress of multi-syllable nouns	• Assess your prior knowledge of content • Relate personal experiences to listening topics • Integrate information from multiple sources • Reflect on what you have learned in the unit • Analyze your attitudes toward culture-based beliefs • Evaluate choices made by others • Combine information from multiple sources	• Participate in a group discussion about bad situations with happy endings.
• Future expressions with *be going to*	• Reduction of *be going to*	• Assess your prior knowledge of content • Relate personal experiences to listening topics • Integrate information from multiple sources • Reflect on what you have learned in the unit • Interpret photographs • Relate your own background to that of others • Assess personal preferences	• Give a presentation describing a tour to a popular travel destination
• Simple present verbs in narratives	• The 3rd person -s ending for simple present verbs	• Assess your prior knowledge of content • Relate personal experiences to listening topics • Integrate information from multiple sources • Reflect on what you have learned in the unit • Examine personal tastes • Evaluate the effectiveness of advice • Speculate about a possible career	• Use appropriate eye contact, tone of voice, and pauses to tell a funny story or a joke to your classmates
• Gerunds as subjects or objects	• Intonation in questions about choices	• Assess your prior knowledge of content • Relate personal experiences to listening topics • Integrate information from multiple sources • Reflect on what you have learned in the unit • Assess personal tastes and habits • Infer ideas from pictures • Classify musical pieces • Select culturally acceptable expressions of opinion	• Participate in a group interview asking and answering questions about how important music is in your lives

UNIT	LISTENING	SPEAKING	VOCABULARY
8 **Honesty** **Q When is honesty important?** **LISTENING 1: Dishonesty In Schools** A TV News Report (Criminology) **LISTENING 2: What's the Right Thing to Do?** Three Conversations (Sociology)	• Predict content • Listen for main ideas • Listen for details • Make inferences to understand a speaker's attitudes • Listen to identify methods of cheating in various circumstances • Listen for numbers to understand percentages and fractions • Identify individual words in rapid speech to improve listening precision	• Take notes to prepare for a presentation or group discussion • Credit sources to identify where information came from • Compose questions and organize them into a survey • Report results of a survey	• Assess your prior knowledge of vocabulary • Understand and use numbers to express percentages and fractions
9 **Life Changes** **Q Is it ever too late to change?** **LISTENING 1: Attitudes about Change** A Group Discussion (Psychology) **LISTENING 2: Tips from a Life Coach** A Radio Call-In Show (Language Studies)	• Predict content • Listen for main ideas • Listen for details • Listen for agreement / disagreement signals to understand opinions • Recognize indirect disagreement to understand a speaker's attitudes • Listen for exact words or phrases to improve your word recognition • Listen for statements of advice to determine what the speaker recommends • Identify individual words to precisely complete statements	• Take notes to prepare for a presentation or group discussion • Use questions to find out whether a listener understands you • Use agreement / disagreement signals to state your opinion • Use target vocabulary to give advice • Explain a sequence of events	• Assess your prior knowledge of vocabulary • Collocations of verbs and nouns
10 **Fear** **Q When is it good to be afraid?** **LISTENING 1: The Science of Fear** A Conference Presentation (Cognitive Psychology) **LISTENING 2: What Are You Afraid of?** A Discussion with a Doctor (Physiology)	• Predict content • Listen for main ideas • Listen for details • Take notes to reflect classifications made in a listening passage • Listen for examples to sort into classifications • Listen for cause-effect relationships in a presentation	• Take notes to prepare for a presentation or group discussion • Show surprise, happiness, and sadness in conversation • Tell a personal story to express fears • Role-play conversations to practice appropriate responses	• Assess your prior knowledge of vocabulary • Idioms and expressions

GRAMMAR	PRONUNCIATION	CRITICAL THINKING	UNIT OUTCOME
• Conjunctions *and* and *but*	• Linkages of consonants to vowels	• Assess your prior knowledge of content • Relate personal experiences to listening topics • Integrate information from multiple sources • Reflect on what you have learned in the unit • Rank actions as right or wrong • Relate personal experience to a topic • Recognize which source deserves credit for information	• Conduct a survey to gather opinions on honesty and dishonesty, and then report your results to the class
• Imperative of *Be* + adjective	• Content word stress in sentences	• Assess your prior knowledge of content • Relate personal experiences to listening topics • Integrate information from multiple sources • Reflect on what you have learned in the unit • Identify personal experiences relevant to a topic • Assess personal reactions to change • Speculate about future circumstances • Examine cultural values	• Deliver a presentation providing instructions on how a person can make a change in his/her life
• *So* and *such* with adjectives	• Linking vowel sounds with /w/ or /y/	• Assess your prior knowledge of content • Relate personal experiences to listening topics • Integrate information from multiple sources • Reflect on what you have learned in the unit • Recognize personal emotions • Analyze photographs • Infer a speaker's attitudes	• Use phrases for expressing emotions to describe a frightening experience

LISTENING	●	listening for examples
VOCABULARY	●	prefixes that mean *not*
GRAMMAR	●	simple present statements and questions
PRONUNCIATION	●	intonation in questions
SPEAKING	●	asking follow-up questions

LEARNING OUTCOME ●

Interview a classmate and introduce him/her to the class using the simple present tense.

Unit QUESTION

Do you like your name?

PREVIEW THE UNIT

A Discuss these questions with your classmates.

What is your full name?

What do most people call you?

Look at the photo. Do you know any of the names?

B Discuss the Unit Question above with your classmates.

🔊 Listen to *The Q Classroom*, **Track 2 on CD 1, to hear other answers.**

3

C Look at the photos. Read them with a partner. Then introduce yourself to your partner.

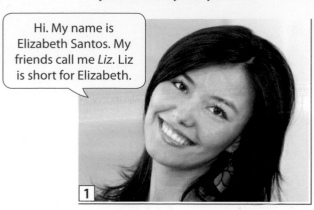

Hi. My name is Elizabeth Santos. My friends call me *Liz*. Liz is short for Elizabeth.

Hi. My name is Janek Novak. My friends call me *Jump* because I like to play basketball.

D Work in a group. Read the information in the chart below about Liz and Jump from Activity C. Then complete the chart with the names of people in your group.

Name I want to be called	Family name (last name)	Given name (first name)	Nickname/s
Liz	Santos	Elizabeth	Liz
Janek	Novak	Janek	Jump

E Discuss these questions in your group.

1. What are some common first names in your country? Last names?

2. What are common nicknames for family members (mother, father, grandmother, grandfather, aunt, uncle, etc.) in your country? How about in other countries?

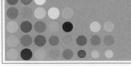
LISTENING 1 | Given Names and Nicknames

VOCABULARY

Tip for Success

Keep a small pocket-sized vocabulary notebook for new words. Review your new words a few times a week.

Here are some words from Listening 1. Read the sentences. Circle the best definition for each bold word.

1. What is your **opinion** of that book? Do you like it?
   a. thought about
   b. name for

2. My nickname is *Bobby*, but at work I go by *Robert*. People think **differently** about me when I use my given name.
   a. the same way
   b. not the same way

3. Some names can describe your **personality**. For example, the Arabic name Akilah means "intelligent."
   a. the interests of a person
   b. the qualities of a person

4. An **honest** person found my money and returned it to me.
   a. always telling the truth
   b. always telling lies

5. I like **friendly** classmates. We can do our homework together.
   a. kind and helpful
   b. sad and serious

6. Tarik has a lot of friends at school. He's very **popular**.
   a. disliked by many people
   b. liked by many people

PREVIEW LISTENING 1

Given Names and Nicknames

You are going to listen to a group of students discuss an article about given names and nicknames.

Look at the photos. The people are introducing themselves. In each situation, is it better to use a given name or a nickname? Check (✓) your answer.

☐ given names   ☐ nicknames   ☐ given names   ☐ nicknames

LISTEN FOR MAIN IDEAS

 CD 1
Track 3

Read the sentences. Then listen to the discussion. Check (✓) the main ideas.

☐ 1. People sometimes change their names.
☐ 2. The way you say your name can change someone's opinion of you.
☐ 3. People connect names with personality.
☐ 4. Names are important for business.
☐ 5. Names in some cultures are very long.

LISTEN FOR DETAILS

CD 1
Track 4

Listen again. Then circle the word or phrase that best completes each statement.

1. Using your given name can make people think that you are (friendly / honest).

2. Using your given name can also make people think you are (successful / serious).

3. Using a nickname makes people think you are (popular / honest).

 **WHAT DO YOU THINK?**

Discuss the questions in a group.

1. In your country, when do you use your given name? Your nickname?

2. Do you agree that a name can change someone's opinion of a person? Why or why not?

3. What is one new thing you learned in Listening 1?

| Listening Skill | Listening for examples | |

Speakers often give **examples** to help explain their ideas. Listening for examples can help you better understand. Here are three expressions speakers use to introduce examples.

- **like:** use after a comma to give examples. *Like* usually comes in the middle of a sentence, or before the last part of a sentence.

  Some people, **like** my family and friends, call me Bob.

  I have nicknames for many people in my life, **like** my mom is "ma" and my dad is "pop."

- **such as:** use after a comma to give examples. *Such as* comes in the middle of a sentence, or before the last part of a sentence.

  In some countries, **such as** Argentina and Peru, people have two or three given names.

  I'd like to live in a Latin American country, **such as** Argentina or Ecuador.

- **for example:** use with a comma before and after it when in the middle of a sentence. *For example* can come at the beginning of a sentence, but *like* and *such as* cannot.

  Many common names have nicknames, **for example,** "Bob" for Robert.

  Names can have meaning. **For example,** Taro means "big boy" in Japanese.

CD 1
Track 5

A. Listen and complete the sentences with the expressions you hear.

1. Some English names have nicknames, _____

   Jen or Tony.

2. In Asian countries, _____ Korea and Japan,

   names have a special meaning.

3. Some people have the same name as another family member,

_____, a parent or a grandparent.

4. In Russia, some family names are very common,

_____ Ivanov or Petrov.

CD 1
Track 6

B. Complete the excerpt of the conversation from Listening 1 with the words and phrases from the box. Then listen and check your answers.

opinion	popular	successful	differently
honest	~~nickname~~	honest	introduce

Hassan: ... Let's talk about the article on names. Can anyone tell me something about it?

Jim: Sure. The article is about given names and nicknames—for example, Tom is a _____nickname_____ for Thomas and Liz for
                                                    1
Elizabeth. It says that the way you say your name can give people

a different _____ about you. For example, when I
                      2

_____ myself with my given name, James, people think
            3

_____ about me than when I use my nickname, Jim.
          4

Emiko: Yes, the article is interesting. It also says that people connect

names with a type of personality, like an _____ personality.
                                                       5

Hassan: Can you say more about that, Emiko?

Emiko: Well, for example, if you use your given name, people think that

you are _____. And using your given name also makes
                    6
people feel that you are _____.
                                    7

Jim: Yes, and if you use your nickname, people think you are friendly or

_____.
        8

Emiko: So, people have a different opinion of you, depending on your name.

Tip for Success

As you continue through this book, review the listening skills from previous units. Practice these new skills as you do the listening exercises in the book.

LISTENING 2 | Stage Names

VOCABULARY

Here are some words from Listening 2. Read the definitions.
Then complete each conversation with the correct word.

> **choose** (*verb*) to decide which thing or person you want
> **famous** (*adjective*) known by many people
> **ordinary** (*adjective*) normal, not special or different
> **pronounce** (*verb*) to make the sound of a letter or word
> **similar** (*adjective*) the same in some ways, but not exactly the same
> **unusual** (*adjective*) interesting because it is different

1. A: My name is difficult to say.

    B: Yes, it is. I can't _____ it very well.

2. A: What's your name?

    B: It's Kaya. It's not very common in the United States.

    A: Yes, that is a(n) _____ name.

3. A: Do you have a nickname?

    B: No, but I want one. My given name is too common.

    A: Yeah, I have a(n) _____ name, too.

4. A: My brother is an actor. But he isn't very well known.

    B: Well, I hope he becomes _____ someday.

5. A: My name is almost the same as my brother's name.

    B: Yes. "Ryan" and "Brian" are very _____.

6. A: Did you _____ a name for your baby yet?

    B: No, not yet. There are so many nice names. It's hard to decide.

PREVIEW LISTENING 2

Stage Names

You are going to listen to a radio talk-show. The host interviews a Hollywood reporter about the names celebrities choose to use.

Do you know these celebrities' real names? Match the pictures to the names.

1 Ringo Starr

2 Miley Cyrus

3 Bruce Lee

___ Lee Zhen Fan

___ Richard Starkey

___ Destiny Hope Cyrus

LISTEN FOR MAIN IDEAS

CD 1
Track 7

Read the statements. Then listen to the interview. Check (✓) the three reasons the reporter says celebrities change their names.

___ 1. They don't like their given names.

___ 2. Their real names are too ordinary.

___ 3. They want a name that is easy to pronounce.

___ 4. They want a name that is similar to another star.

___ 5. They want an unusual name.

___ 6. They don't want people to know them.

LISTEN FOR DETAILS

CD 1
Track 8

Read the questions. Listen again and choose the correct answer for each.

1. Why did Ringo Starr change his name?
   a. He couldn't remember his name.
   b. He wanted a new family name.
   c. He wanted an unusual name.

2. What star wanted a name that was easy to pronounce?
   a. Bruce Lee
   b. Miley Cyrus
   c. Ringo Starr

3. When did Bruce Lee change his name?
   a. When he became an international star
   b. When he moved to China
   c. When he was a child

4. Which star uses a nickname?
   a. Bruce Lee
   b. Miley Cyrus
   c. Stella Skye

5. What advice does Stella give for choosing a stage name?
   a. Choose a name you like.
   b. Choose a short name.
   c. Choose a name that's similar to your name.

 **WHAT DO YOU THINK?**

A. Discuss the questions in a group.

1. What are other reasons people change their names?

2. Do you want to change your name? Why or why not?

B. Think about both Listening 1 and Listening 2 as you discuss the questions.

1. Who are your favorite celebrities? Do you think their names are important? Why or why not?

2. Think of a good nickname or stage name for yourself. What does it mean?

Vocabulary Skill | **Prefixes that mean *not***

A **prefix** is a letter or a group of letters at the beginning of a word. Prefixes change the meaning of a word. The prefixes *dis-*, *in-*, and *un-* mean *not*. They give a word the opposite meaning.

like →	**dis**like (not like)
formal →	**in**formal (not formal)
usual →	**un**usual (not usual)

Learning the meaning of prefixes will help you build your vocabulary.

A. Complete the chart. Add *dis-*, *in-*, or *un-* to create the opposite meaning of each word. Use your dictionary to help you.

Word	Opposite meaning	Word	Opposite meaning
active	*inactive*	expensive	
agree		friendly	
convenient	inconvenient	honest	
correct		popular	

B. Complete the conversations with the opposite meanings from Activity A.

1. **A:** Do you spell your name A-L-A-N?

   B: No, sorry, that's _____incorrect_____. It's A-L-L-E-N.

2. **A:** I think it's OK to use nicknames for business.

   B: Really? I _____. I think it's much too informal.

3. **A:** I got married last month. Now I have a new family name, so I need to change my documents... I have to change everything!

   B: Wow! I never thought about that. That's very _____.

4. **A:** Why are some names so _____?

   B: Maybe because they're just hard to spell or pronounce.

5. **A:** Did you hear that the volcano near my house erupted last week?

   B: No, that's surprising. It was _____ for many years, wasn't it?

6. **A:** Do you ever buy famous brand name clothes?

   B: No, I usually buy _____ clothing.

7. **A:** The new student is very ___ _____. She never smiles.

   B: Maybe she's just shy.

8. **A:** One of my classmates copies his school reports from the Internet.

   B: Oh, that's really _____.

SPEAKING

- Use the simple present to talk about facts, definitions, or general truths.

  Mei **means** "pretty" in Chinese.   China **is** a big country.

- Use the simple present to describe habits or routines, or things that happen again and again.

  Mei and her brother **don't drive** to work.   They **take** the train.

- Use the simple present to describe states and feelings (with verbs such as *be*, *have*, and *like*).

  Mei **has** a cat.   She **likes** celebrities.

Simple present statements with regular verbs

Affirmative		Negative	
I You	**like** celebrities.	I You	**do not like** celebrities.
He She It	**eats** only vegetables.	He She It	**does not eat** meat.
We You They	**live** in a big city.	We You They	**do not live** in a small town.

Simple present statements with *be*

Affirmative		Negative	
I	**am** friendly.	I	**am not** mean.
You	**are** a celebrity.	You	**are not** popular.
He She It	**is** at work.	He She It	**is not** at home.
We You They	**are** actors.	We You They	**are not** famous.

Simple present statements with *have*

Affirmative	Negative
I You **have** an interesting name.	I You **do not have** a nickname.
He She **has** a long name. It	He She **does not have** a short name. It
We You **have** stage names. They	We You **do not have** stage names. They

Note: Contractions (short forms) with *be* and *do* are common in informal written language and in spoken language.

Affirmative			Negative		
I am	=	I'm	I am not	=	I'm not
is	=	's	is not	=	isn't
are	=	're	are not	=	aren't or 're not
			do not	=	don't
			does not	=	doesn't

A. Circle the correct verb form to complete each sentence.

1. English names (is / **are**) popular in countries such as Thailand and China.

2. I (has / **have**) a nickname, but for business I (**use** / uses) my given name.

3. His real name (**is** / are) Richard Starkey, but everyone (call / **calls**)
   him Ringo.

4. In my country, women (**don't** / doesn't) change their family names when
   they (**get** / gets) married.

5. Katerina (don't / **doesn't**) like her name. She (think / **thinks**) it's difficult
   to pronounce.

6. Beyoncé (**isn't** / aren't) a stage name. (**It's** / They're) the singer's real name.

B. Write the simple present form of each verb.

My name ___is___ Felicidad Montoya. I ___don't have___ [1. (be)] [2. (not have)]
a nickname. My family name ___isn't___ very common. My first [3. (not be)]
name ___mean___ "happiness" in English. I ___am___ [4. (mean)] [5. (be)]
from Lima, Peru. I ___have___ one brother and two sisters. My [6. (have)]
sisters ___live___ near me, but my brother ___doesn't lives___ [7. (live)] [8. (not live)]
here. He ___has___ a job in Brazil. He ___works___ [9. (have)] [10. (work)]
at a bank. My sister's name ___is___ Federica, but she [11. (be)]
___doesn't likes___ her name. We usually ___call___ her [12. (not like)] [13. (call)]
"Rica." She ___likes___ that nickname better. My younger sister [14. (like)]
___doesn't have___ a nickname, but she doesn't mind. [15. (not have)]

Grammar | *Part 2* **Simple present questions**

Yes/No questions

Regular Verbs			Be		
Do	I	**know** you?	**Am**	I	correct?
	you	**like** celebrities?	**Are**	you	OK?
Does	he	**eat** meat?	**Is**	he	a vegetarian?
	she	**have** a nickname?		she	from Brazil?
	it	**look** OK?		it	correct?
Do	we	**have** time to study?	**Are**	we	in a group?
	you	**have** nicknames?		you	students?
	they	**work** in the city?		they	partners?

Information questions

Regular Verbs			Be		
How do	I you	**know** you? **like** your name?	**Where**	am are	I? you?
Where does	he she it	**live**? **study** English? **belong**?	**How**	is	he? she? it?
What do	we you they	**call** him? **want** to discuss? **like** to do?	**Where**	are	you from? we? they?

A. Form questions. Use the words.

1. name / like / do / you / your

   Do you like your name _____ ?

2. your / is / actor / who / favorite

   who is your favorite actor _____ ?

3. your / where / does / work / sister

   where does your sister work _____ ?

4. impolite / it / to use / nickname / your / is / work / at

   Is it impolite to use your nickname at work _____ ?

5. your / does / in English / something / name / mean

   does your name something mean in English _____ ?

6. want / she / her / to change / does / why / name

   why she wants to change her name _____ ?

7. celebrities / why / use / do / stage names

   why celebrities do use stage names _____ ?

8. is / common / family name / your

   is your family name common _____ ?

B. Choose five questions from Activity A. Ask and answer them with a partner.

| Pronunciation | Intonation in *yes/no* and information questions | web+ |

Yes/No Questions

Questions that have a *yes* or *no* answer usually have rising intonation at the end of the question. The voice goes up.

CD 1
Track 9

Listen to these examples.

Are you Mark Johnson?   Does she have a stage name?

Information Questions

Questions that begin with a question word (*who*, *what*, *where*, *when*, *why*, or *how*) usually have falling intonation at the end. The voice goes down.

CD 1
Track 10

Listen to these examples.

What is your family name?   Why do people change their names?

CD 1
Track 11

A. Listen and repeat the questions. Use the same intonation you hear.

1. What is your family name?

2. Do you have a nickname?

3. Where are you from?

4. Where do you live now?

5. Is your family name common?

6. Do you have any brothers?
   I am an only children

7. Why do you like your name?

8. Does it rain a lot where you come from?

B. Work with a partner. Take turns asking and answering the questions in Activity A. Use the correct intonation for each type of question.

Follow-up questions are questions that ask for more information. You can ask follow-up questions to keep a conversation going.

> **A:** Are you interested in sports?
>
> **B:** Yes, I like baseball.
>
> **A: Oh, what's your favorite team?**
>
> **B:** I like the Seattle Mariners.
>
> **A: Do you have a favorite player?**

Asking follow-up questions helps make your conversations more interesting, and helps you learn more about people you meet.

A. Read the information in Sanjay and Anita's profiles. Then complete their conversation below by writing Sanjay's follow-up questions.

Sanjay Patel

Hometown
Mumbai, India

Favorite music
alternative rock, especially 00s music

Interests
computer games and traveling

Interesting fact
name means "winner" in English

Anita Gomez

Hometown
Mexico City, Mexico

Favorite music
hip-hop bands, especially the Black Eyed Peas

Interests
art and mountain biking

Interesting fact
family name is common in Mexico

Sanjay: Hi, I'm Sanjay.

Anita: It's nice to meet you, Sanjay. I'm Anita.

Sanjay: Where ___are you from___ , Anita?

Anita: I'm from Mexico...from Mexico City.

Sanjay: Is Mexico City ___a big city___?

Anita: Yes, it's very big. About 8,000,000 people live there.

Sanjay: Is your family name ___common___?

Anita: Yes, it's very common there. My first name is common, too.

Sanjay: Does your first name ___mean anything___?

Anita: Yes, it means "Little Ana." It comes from my grandmother's name.

Sanjay: I see. So, what kind of ___music do you like___? or listen to

Anita: Well, I listen to a lot of hip-hop music.

Sanjay: Oh, really? What's ___you favorite group___? or band

Anita: The Black Eyed Peas.

Sanjay: They're pretty good. So, what are your ___interest___?

Anita: Well, I like mountain biking, and I'm really interested in art.

B. With your partner, write a conversation where Anita asks Sanjay follow-up questions. Then take turns reading the conversation out loud.

Unit Assignment | **Make an introduction**

 In this assignment, you will introduce a classmate and tell some interesting information about him or her. As you prepare your introduction, think about the Unit Question, "Do you like your name?" and refer to the Self-Assessment checklist on page 22.

For alternative unit assignments, see the *Q: Skills for Success Teacher's Handbook.*

CONSIDER THE IDEAS

Read Sanjay's introduction of Anita. Check (✓) the information he includes.

I'd like to meet my friend

"Good morning. I'd like to introduce my friend Anita Gomez. Her given name comes from her grandmother's name, Ana. Anita means "little Ana" in English. She likes that name. She thinks it's pretty. Anita is from Mexico City, Mexico. Mexico City is a very big city with many people, and it is an interesting place to visit. Anita's favorite music is hip-hop, and she loves the Black Eyed Peas. Anita likes to go mountain biking..."

____ 1. what *Anita* means in English

____ 2. Anita's hometown

____ 3. the meaning of Anita's family name

____ 4. where Anita lives now

____ 5. information about Mexico City

____ 6. sports Anita enjoys

____ 7. Anita's favorite music

PREPARE AND SPEAK

A. **GATHER IDEAS** Work in a group. Look at the topics in the box. Together, think of questions you can ask someone when you first meet him or her. In your notebook, write <u>two questions</u> for each topic in the box.

| Name | Family | Hometown | Interests | Favorites |

B. **ORGANIZE IDEAS** You will interview a partner to learn information about him or her. Write your two questions from Activity A for each topic in the chart.

siblings

Topics	Questions	My Partner's Answers
Name	what does your name mean? do you like you name? is family name common in your country?	Meaning: Wahla is tree dry need water El Ellaghi is common
Family	how many people are in your family? do you have any brothers or sisters?	Seven family Dad, Mom brother ① sister ④
Hometown	where were you born? is a big and nice city	Tripoly is a capital of libia Tripoly has a many buildings close to close
Interests	what are your interests? how often do you do it?	cook → international food. coskos arabic food every day
Favorites	what are your favorite sports? who is your favorite movie star?	walking Jennifer Lopez actris susician

C. SPEAK **Work with a partner. Refer to the Self-Assessment checklist below before you begin.**

verb
noun

1. Interview your partner using your questions from the chart in Activity B. Remember to ask follow-up questions. Write your partner's answers in your notebook.

2. Now introduce your partner to a group or to the class. Use your notes from Activity B.

CHECK AND REFLECT

A. CHECK **Think about the Unit Assignment as you complete the Self-Assessment checklist.**

SELF-ASSESSMENT		
Yes	**No**	
☒	☐	I was able to speak easily about the topic.
☒	☐	My partner/group/class understood me.
☐	☐	I used the simple present in statements and questions.
☐	☐	I used vocabulary from the unit.
☐	☐	I used follow-up questions correctly.
☐	☐	I used proper intonation in questions.

B. REFLECT **Discuss these questions with a partner.**

What is something new you learned in this unit?

 Think about the Unit Question, "Do you like your name?" How do you feel about your name now? The same or different? Explain.

Circle the words you learned in this unit.

Nouns
opinion 🗝
personality 🗝

Verbs
choose 🗝
pronounce

Adjectives
famous 🗝
friendly 🗝
honest 🗝
ordinary 🗝
popular 🗝
similar 🗝 AWL
unusual 🗝

Adverb
differently

different → noun
My mom and I do things differently

🗝 Oxford 2000 keywords
AWL Academic Word List
For more information on the Oxford 2000 keywords and the AWL, see page xi

Phrases and Expressions
for example
such as

Prepositions
like 🗝

Check (✓) the skills you learned. If you need more work on a skill, refer to the page(s) in parentheses.

LISTENING ⚪	I can listen for examples. (p. 7)
VOCABULARY ⚪	I can recognize and use prefixes that mean *not*. (p. 12)
GRAMMAR ⚪	I can recognize and use the simple present. (pp. 14–17)
PRONUNCIATION ⚪	I can understand and use intonation in questions. (p. 18)
SPEAKING ⚪	I can ask follow-up questions. (p. 19)
LEARNING OUTCOME ⚫	I can interview a classmate and introduce him/her to the class using the simple present tense.

LISTENING	●	listening for key words and phrases
VOCABULARY	●	using the dictionary
GRAMMAR	●	simple past
PRONUNCIATION	●	simple past -*ed* endings
SPEAKING	●	asking for repetition and clarification

LEARNING OUTCOME

Write interview questions
and role-play a job
interview.

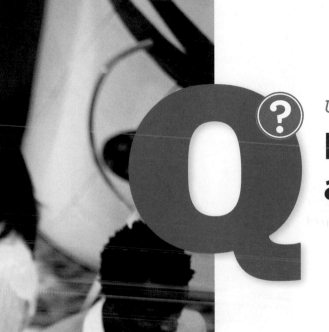

Unit QUESTION

How can you find a good job?

PREVIEW THE UNIT

A Discuss these questions with your classmates.

Do you have a job?

What is your dream job?

Look at the photo. Where are these people?
What are they doing?

B Discuss the Unit Question above with your classmates.

Listen to *The Q Classroom*, Track 12 on CD 1, to hear other answers.

C Match the ads to the jobs in the photos. More than one answer is possible.

1 tempor incididunt ut labore et dolore

Must have excellent computer skills

2 labora et dolore

Need a college education

Email resume to:

3 Need three years of experience

4 skills. One to two years of experience years of

Must have a friendly personality

Must be organized. Need excellent

Website designer _1 - 2 - 3_

Salesperson _4_

Server _4_

Teacher _3, 2, 1_

D Tell your partner which job you like best, and why.

A: I like the website designer job. I have excellent computer skills.

B: Really? I prefer the salesperson position. I like working with people.

LISTENING 1 | Looking for a Job

VOCABULARY

Here are some words from Listening 1. Read the sentences. Then write each bold word next to the correct definition.

1. Paul wants to change his **career**. He wants to become a nurse.

2. Kim starts her new job tomorrow. She's a new **employee** in that company.

3. A college education is one **requirement** to be a teacher. You also need some teaching experience.

4. I don't know much about computers. I can only do **basic** things, like type papers and use email.

5. Our server isn't very **organized**. He forgot to bring your coffee, and he brought me the wrong food.

6. Education is important. It's harder to get some jobs if you don't have a college **degree**.

7. I want to get a job at Rick's Café. I just have to complete this **application** and take it to the restaurant.

8. I have an **interview** next week at a computer company.

a. _employee_ (*noun*) a person who works for someone

b. _degree_ (*noun*) a paper you get when you finish university

c. _career_ (*noun*) a job that you learn to do and then do for many years

d. _application_ (*noun*) a special piece of paper you fill out when you try to get a job

e. _requirement_ (*noun*) something that you need or that you must do or have

f. _organized_ (*adjective*) able to plan your work or life well

g. _interview_ (*noun*) a meeting when someone asks you questions to decide if you will get a job

h. _basic_ (*adjective*) simple; including only what is necessary

PREVIEW LISTENING 1

Looking for a Job

Two students are looking online for a summer job. They find a Website with a video called "Careers at Braxton Books."

Check (✓) the topics you think the video will include.

☐ how to buy books online   ☑ how to get an application

☑ job requirements   ☐ store hours

LISTEN FOR MAIN IDEAS

🔊 CD 1
Track 13

Read the statements. Then listen to the conversation. Write *T* (true) or *F* (false).

_F_ 1. Sarah works at Braxton Books now.

_T_ 2. Braxton Books is a big company.

_T_ 3. The company sells books in stores and online.

_T_ 4. The company has some open jobs.

_T_ 5. Sarah will probably try to get a job at Braxton Books.

LISTEN FOR DETAILS

🔊 CD 1
Track 14

Read the job requirements. Then listen to the excerpt from Listening 1. Check (✓) the requirements for each job.

> **Tip for Success**
>
> Speakers sometimes use certain phrases to signal a list of important information. Some examples are:
> *Here are... /*
> *The following are... /*
> *Here is a list of...*

Requirements	Salesperson	Web designer
1. must have experience	✓ 1 or 2 years	✓ 5 years
2. must have excellent computer skills	\	\
3. must have a college degree		\
4. must be friendly	\	
5. must be organized	\	\

Integrals

 **WHAT DO YOU THINK?**

Tip Critical Thinking

Question 1 asks you to **compare** the two jobs. **Comparing** means you notice the things that are the same for both jobs. Comparing can help you remember important points about the two things.

Discuss the questions in a group.

1. Look again at the chart. What requirements are necessary for both jobs?

2. Do you meet the requirements for the jobs? Which ones?

3. Which student in your group is the best person for each job at Braxton Books?

| Listening Skill | Listening for key words and phrases | |

Key words and phrases tell you the important information about a topic. Speakers often repeat key words and phrases more than once. Listening for key words and phrases can help you identify the topic of a conversation.

CD 1
Track 15

Listen to the example from Listening 1.

The topic of the conversation is *looking for a summer job*.

The key words and phrases are: *work there this summer, jobs, careers*. The speakers say the words *summer* and *job* more than once.

CD 1
Track 16

A. Sarah and Sehoon are listening to the information video for Braxton Books. Listen for key words and phrases in each section. Circle the main topic.

1. a. careers at Braxton Books
   b. the company's history and success
   c. the number of employees

2. a. jobs at Braxton Books
   b. how to get an application
   c. job interviews

3. a. store hours
   b. computer skills
   c. job requirements

4. a. job interviews
   b. how to get an application
   c. how to buy online books

B. Listen again. Check (✓) the words and phrases the speaker uses <u>more than once</u>.

1. ☐ interest in careers
   ☐ growing
   ☐ two hundred stores
   ☐ success

3. ☐ requirements
   ☐ college degree
   ☐ years of experience
   ☐ interesting

2. ☐ job
   ☐ position
   ☐ great people
   ☐ join our team

4. ☐ interested
   ☐ one of our stores
   ☐ application
   ☐ interview

LISTENING 2 | The Right Person for the Job

VOCABULARY

Here are some words from Listening 2. Read the definitions. Then complete each sentence below with the correct word.

> **advertising** (*noun*) telling people about things to buy
> **assistant** (*noun*) a person who helps someone in a more important position
> **graduate** (*verb*) to finish your studies at a school, college, or university
> **major** (*noun*) the main subject you study in college
> **manager** (*noun*) the person who controls a company or a business
> **resume** (*noun*) a list of your education and work experience that you send when you are trying to get a new job

1. My mother speaks French very well. French was her _____major_____ in college.

2. Juan got a job as a(n) _____assistant_____ in a school. He'll help the children when the teacher is busy.

3. It isn't easy to get a job in _____advertising_____. You need to have interesting ideas, and you have to know how to sell things.

4. I sent my _____resume_____ to ten companies. Only one company called me for an interview.

5. My father is the ___manager___ of a large restaurant. He has a lot of employees, and he's very busy.

6. I plan to ___graduate___ from college next year.

Tip for Success

Remember to listen for the key words and phrases. They will help you know the topics of the interview.

PREVIEW LISTENING 2

The Right Person for the Job

You are going to listen to Margaret Williamson, the manager of New World Design Advertising Company. She is going to interview Tom and Wendy for a Web designer position.

Check (✓) the interview questions you think Margaret will ask.

1. ☑ Can you tell me a little about yourself?
2. ☑ What was your major in college?
   ☐ How old are you?
3. ☑ Do you have any experience in advertising?
4. ☑ What are your best qualities?
   ☐ Are you married?
5. ☑ Do you have any questions?

[handwritten notes: 4 more inside; a hard worker; a team player ⇒ I work well with other people; good at solving problems; helpful, considerate; think quickly on my feet; qualities →]

LISTEN FOR MAIN IDEAS

CD 1 Track 18

Listen to the interviews. Check (✓) the <u>two</u> topics each person talks about.

	Education	Experience	Skills
1. Tom			
2. Wendy			

LISTEN FOR DETAILS

CD 1 Track 19

Read the sentences. Then listen again. Circle the word or phrase that best completes each sentence.

1. The company is in (New York / Chicago).

2. Tom (studied / didn't study) art in college.

3. Tom has (some / no) experience in advertising.

4. Tom worked at a (convenience store / restaurant) in college.

5. Wendy has (a little / a lot of) experience in Web design.

6. Wendy likes working (alone / with others).

 **WHAT DO YOU THINK?**

A. Discuss the questions in a group.

1. Which person should get the job? Why?

   A: I think...should get the job...   She has...   He has...
   B: I disagree. I think...

2. Are job interviews the same in your country? What questions do people ask?

B. Think about both Listening 1 and Listening 2 as you discuss the questions.

1. Discuss the steps you take to find a job in the U.S. Are these steps the same in your country?

2. With your group, think of three interesting jobs. List some requirements for each job. Which requirements does each group member meet?

| Vocabulary Skill | Using the dictionary | |

Some **words have similar meanings**, but they are used in different situations. The definitions and the example sentences in the dictionary can help you decide which word is best to use.

Look at the dictionary entries and example sentences for *career* and *work*.

---

ca·reer 🔑 /kəˈrɪr/ *noun* [*count*]
a job that you learn to do and then do for many years: *He is considering a **career** in teaching.* ◆ *His career was always more important to him than his family.* ➲ Look at the note at **job**.

work² 🔑 /wərk/ *noun*
1 [*noncount*] the job that you do to earn money: *I'm looking for work* ◆ *What time do you **start work**?* ◆ *How long have you been **out of work** (= without a job)?* ➲ Look at the note at **job**.

> Max graduated from college last year. He's ready to start a **career**.
> I have to leave for **work** very early tomorrow morning.

The definition of *career*, as you can see, is a job you want or plan to do for a long time. *Work* is a more general word meaning the job you do for money.

Always look for both words in the dictionary before deciding which one to use.

A. Read the dictionary entries and circle the best word for each sentence.

job 🔑 **AWL** /dʒɑb/ *noun* [*count*]
1 the work that you do for money: *She got a job as a waitress.* • *Peter just lost his job.*

ca·reer 🔑 /kəˈrɪr/ *noun* [*count*]
a job that you learn to do and then do for many years: *He is considering a career in teaching.* • *His career was always more important to him than his family.* ↪ Look at the note at **job**.

1. A (job / **career**) in law can be very demanding.

2. My company closed. I need to find another (**job** / career) soon.

com·pa·ny 🔑 /ˈkʌmpəni/ *noun* (plural **com·pa·nies**)
1 [*count*] (**BUSINESS**) a group of people who work together to make or sell things: *an advertising company* • *the Student Loans Company* ↪ The short way of writing "Company" in names is Co.: *Milton and Co.*
2 [*noncount*] being with a person or people: *I always enjoy Mark's company.*

busi·ness 🔑 /ˈbɪznəs/ *noun* (plural **busi·ness·es**)
1 [*noncount*] buying and selling things: *I want to go into business when I leave school.* • *Business is not very good this year.*
2 [*noncount*] the work that you do as your job: *The manager will be away on business next week.* • *a business trip*

3. Jim went into (company / **business**) with his brother.

4. The (**company** / business) has over 6,000 employees around the world.

B. Write one new sentence for each word in Activity A.

1. (job) _I need an extra job for summer time._

2. (career) _My career in Accounton is very demanding in canada._

3. (company) _I want to work in a big company._

4. (business) _My husband and I want to open our own business._

SPEAKING

Use the **simple past** to talk about actions that happened in the past.

Regular Verbs

- To form the simple past, add -*ed* to the base form of the verb.

  > I work**ed** at a clothing store last summer. I help**ed** customers.

- For words ending in *e*, add -*d*.

  > I serv**ed** lunch and dinner at a busy restaurant. I also prepare**d** take-out orders.

- For words ending in *y*, drop the *y* and add -*ied*.

  > Tom app**lied** for a position as a Web designer. He stud**ied** Web design in college.

Irregular Verbs

The verb *be* is irregular in the simple past. It has two forms: *was* and *were*.

> My internship **was** a good experience. The people I worked with **were** great.

Here are some other verbs with irregular simple past forms.

say	**said**	know	**knew**
make	**made**	take	**took**
go	**went**	come	**came**
do	**did**	see	**saw**
have	**had**	get	**got**

Negative Statements

- To form a negative statement, use *didn't* + base form of the verb.

  > I **didn't graduate** from high school last year. It was two years ago.

Questions

- To form a question, use (*wh*-word) + *did* + subject + base form of the verb.

  > **Did** you **get** the job?   **What did** you **major** in?

- For questions with the verb *be*, use (*wh*-word) + *was* or *were* + subject.

  > **How was** the interview?   **Were** you ready for all of the questions?

A. Complete each sentence with the simple past form of the verb.

Margaret: Well, let's get started. Please sit down, Tom… OK. Can you tell me a little about yourself?

Tom: Sure. I ___came___ to New York a few months ago from
1. (come)

Chicago. I ___went___ to Chicago School of Design.
2. (go)

Margaret: Yes, I ___saw___ that on your resume. Yes, here it is.
3. (see)

You ___graduated___ last May. What did you study there?
4. (graduate)

Tom: I'm sorry. I didn't catch that. Could you say that again, please?

Margaret: Sure. What ___did___ your major in college?
5. (be)

Tom: Well, I ___got___ my degree in art. I ___took___
6. (get)   7. (take)

a lot of computer classes, too. I ___wanted___ to use my art and
8. (want)

computer skills. That's why I want a career in Web design.

Margaret: OK, Wendy. Please have a seat. Let's see…your resume says

you have some experience in advertising. Tell me about that. Did you

___liked___ it?
9. (like)

Wendy: Oh, yes. It ___was___ a great experience. I
10. (be)

___worked___ in a small advertising company last summer.
11. (work)

I really ___enjoyed___ it. I was an assistant in the office. I
12. (enjoy)

___didn't___ much Web design work—only a little. But I
13. (not do)

___learned___ a lot from my co-workers. I'm excited to learn
14. (learn)

more about it.

Margaret: OK, that's excellent, Wendy. Did you ___studied___ art or
15. (study)

computers in college?

Wendy: No. My major ___was___ English. I ___didn't have___
16. (be)   17. (not have)

a lot of time for other classes.

B. Practice the conversations in Activity A with a partner.

C. Read the notes an interviewer wrote about Carlos. Then read the interview questions below. Write notes in your notebook with your answers. Use the simple past when necessary.

> 1. from Caracas, Venezuela; graduated from Central University in 2009
>
> 2. major was computer science, studied English...
>
> 3. was a Web designer for one year; before that, was a waiter

1. Can you tell me a little about yourself?

2. What did you study in high school/college?

3. What work experience do you have?

D. Take turns asking and answering the job interview questions in Activity C with your partner. Use your notes.

Pronunciation | **Simple past -ed**

The simple past of a regular verb ends in *-ed*. The pronunciation of this final sound depends on the sound at the end of the base verb. There are three possible sounds.

- The *-ed* = /d/ when the sound is **voiced** (with sound). This includes all vowel sounds, and the consonants: /b/, /g/, /dʒ/ (ju**dg**ed), /l/, /m/, /n/, /r/, /v/, and /z/.

- The *-ed* = /t/ when the sound is **unvoiced** (without sound), including /f/, /k/, /p/, /s/, /ʃ/ (wi**sh**), and /tʃ/ (wat**ch**).

- The *-ed* = /əd/ when the final sound is either the voiced sound /d/ or the unvoiced sound /t/.

Read and listen to the examples in the chart.

If the verb ends in...	Base verb	Simple past
a voiced sound, pronounce the past with /d/	enjoy study learn	enjoy**ed** stud**ied** learn**ed**
an unvoiced sound, pronounce the past with /t/	laugh work help wash	laugh**ed** work**ed** help**ed** wash**ed**
a /t/ or /d/, pronounce the past with /əd/	graduate end	graduat**ed** end**ed**

A. Work with a partner. Take turns saying the simple past forms of the verbs in the box.

change	like	need	require	study	walk
complete	look	prefer	stop	wait	want

B. Write the simple past form of each verb in Activity A in the correct column. Listen and check your answers.

/t/	/d/	/əd/
	changed	

C. Read the conversations and <u>underline</u> the regular verbs in the simple past. Write /d/, /t/, or /əd/ above each to tell its correct pronunciation.

1. A: I <u>completed</u> an application for a job at Jim's Pizza today.
           /əd/

    B: Oh, I worked at Jim's Pizza last summer. I washed dishes there. It was fun.

    A: Really? That's good. I wanted to work at Paul's Café, but they said I needed more experience.

    B: Yeah, they chose someone else for the job.

    A: Who?

    B: Me.

2. A: Please sit down, Mr. Smith. Did you bring your application?

    B: Oh, no. I completed it online, and I emailed it. Is that OK?

    A: Oh, yes. Here it is. I printed it this morning... OK. Can you tell me a little about yourself?

    B: Yes, I graduated from Franklin High School in 2010. I wanted to get some work experience before college. So, I joined a computer training program.

    A: I see. Did you finish the program?

    B: Yes, I finished it last week.

D. Practice the conversations in Activity C with your partner. Check your partner's pronunciation of the simple past.

Speaking Skill	Asking for repetition and clarification	

When you listen, sometimes you need to ask the speaker to repeat information. Here are some phrases you can use when you don't hear or understand something well.

I'm sorry… I didn't catch that.	Could you say that again, please?
Could you repeat that?	Do you mean… ?

A. Listen to the excerpt from Listening 2. Check (✓) the phrases Tom uses.

☐ I didn't catch that.
☐ Could you repeat that?
☐ Could you say that again, please?
☐ Do you mean... ?

B. Listen and complete each conversation with a phrase for repetition and clarification.

Michael: Hello?

Susan: Hello, is this Michael Lu?

Michael: Yes, it is.

Susan: Oh, hi, Michael. It's Susan Barden from All-Tech Computers. Thank you for coming to the interview this morning. I forgot to ask you about...

Michael: Hello? _____.

Interviewer: ...Great. OK, thanks. And can you tell me a little about your experience in Australia? I saw on your resume that you...

Linda: _____?

Min-Hee: Hi, Jared. How are you doing?

Jared: Oh, hi, Min-Hee. I'm great! I just found out that...

Min-Hee: Sorry, Jared. _____?

Amber: What do you plan to do after you graduate, Seth?

Seth: Well, I had a meeting with the manager of New World Designs last week.

Amber: A meeting? _____?

C. Take turns reading the conversations in Activity B with a partner.

Tip for Success

It may be impolite in some cultures, but it's important to ask for clarification in English speaking countries when you don't understand something. Begin with *I'm sorry* or *Excuse me* to be more polite.

In this assignment, you are going to write your own interview questions and role-play a job interview with a partner. As you prepare for your role-play, think about the Unit Question, "How can you find a good job?" and refer to the Self-Assessment checklist on page 42.

For alternative unit assignments, see the *Q: Skills for Success Teacher's Handbook*.

CONSIDER THE IDEAS

Work with a partner. Complete the activities.

A. Match each job to the correct advertisement.

___E___ 1. office assistant

___B___ 2. tour guide

___C___ 3. video game tester

___D___ 4. children's sports coach

___F___ 5. house painter

___A___ 6. high school English teacher

A Must have college degree in teaching and two years of experience working in a school.
www.QHS_K-12edu

HELP WANTED

B Must be friendly and organized. Excellent speaking skills.
Must speak English, French, and Spanish.

Email résumé to:
jo@citytours.com

C **Requirements:** excellent computer skills, online game experience.
www.game-on.org

D Experience playing soccer, baseball, and basketball. Must be very friendly.

Complete an application at
www.sports4kidz.org

E Must be organized. Need excellent computer skills. One to two years of experience.
Come in to the office and complete an application. 215 Green Street

F **NO EXPERIENCE NEEDED.**
Must enjoy working outdoors on big projects.
For applications, call (802) 555-2191

B. Read the ads again. Underline the job requirements for each.

C. Work in a group. Which jobs in Activity A do you want to have? Do you meet the requirements? Tell your group.

I want to be an office assistant. I'm organized and have good computer skills.

PREPARE AND SPEAK

A. `GATHER IDEAS` Work with a partner. Think of a job you want to have. Together list the requirements for that job and your partner's job in your notebook.

B. `ORGANIZE IDEAS` Imagine you are going to an interview for your job from Activity A. The interviewer asks you these questions. How do you answer?

1. Can you tell me a little about yourself? _____

_____

2. What did you study in high school or college? _____

_____

3. What work experience do you have? _____

_____

4. What skills do you have? _____

_____

5. Do you have any questions? _____

_____

C. **SPEAK** Role-play the interview with your partner. Refer to the Self-Assessment checklist below before you begin.

A: Hello, I'm _____. Please have a seat.

B: Thank you. It's nice to meet you, _____.

A: OK. Let's get started…(Question 1) _____

B: (Answer) _____

A: (Question 2) _____

B: (Answer) _____

A: _____

B: _____

A: _____

CHECK AND REFLECT

A. **CHECK** Think about the Unit Assignment as you complete the Self-Assessment checklist.

SELF-ASSESSMENT		
Yes	No	
☐	☐	I was able to speak easily about the topic.
☐	☐	My partner/group/class understood me.
☐	☐	I used the simple past.
☐	☐	I used vocabulary from the unit.
☐	☐	I asked for clarification.
☐	☐	I pronounced the simple past of regular verbs.

B. **REFLECT** Discuss these questions with a partner.

What is something new you learned in this unit?

 Think about the Unit Question, "How can you find a good job?" Do you have more answers now than when you started this unit? If yes, what new answers do you have?

Track Your Success

Circle the words you learned in this unit.

Nouns
advertising
application
assistant AWL
career 🔑
degree 🔑
employee
interview 🔑
major AWL
manager 🔑
requirement AWL
resume

Verbs
graduate

Adjectives
basic 🔑
organized 🔑

Phrases
Could you repeat that?
Could you say that
   again, please?
Do you mean... ?
I'm sorry... I didn't
   catch that.

🔑 Oxford 2000 keywords
AWL Academic Word List

Check (✓) the skills you learned. If you need more work on a skill, refer to the page(s) in parentheses.

LISTENING	○ I can listen for key words and phrases. (p. 29)
VOCABULARY	○ I can use the dictionary to help with words with similar meanings. (p. 32)
GRAMMAR	○ I can recognize and use the simple past. (p. 34)
PRONUNCIATION	○ I can pronounce simple past ed endings. (p. 36–37)
SPEAKING	○ I can ask for repetition and clarification. (p. 38)
LEARNING OUTCOME	○ I can write interview questions and role-play a job interview.

UNIT 3

Long Distance

LISTENING	●	taking notes in a T-chart
VOCABULARY	●	guessing words in context
GRAMMAR	●	*should* and *shouldn't* and *It's* + (*not*) adjective + infinitive
PRONUNCIATION	●	the schwa /ə/ sound
SPEAKING	●	presenting information from notes

Give a presentation about customs in a culture you know well.

Unit QUESTION

Why do we study other cultures?

PREVIEW THE UNIT

A Discuss these questions with your classmates.

Did you ever spend time in another country or culture?

What are some things that your country is famous for?

Look at the photo. What do you think the people are talking about?

B Discuss the Unit Question above with your classmates.

Listen to *The Q Classroom*, Track 24 on CD 1, to hear other answers.

C What are some things that make your culture different from other cultures? Write your ideas in the chart.

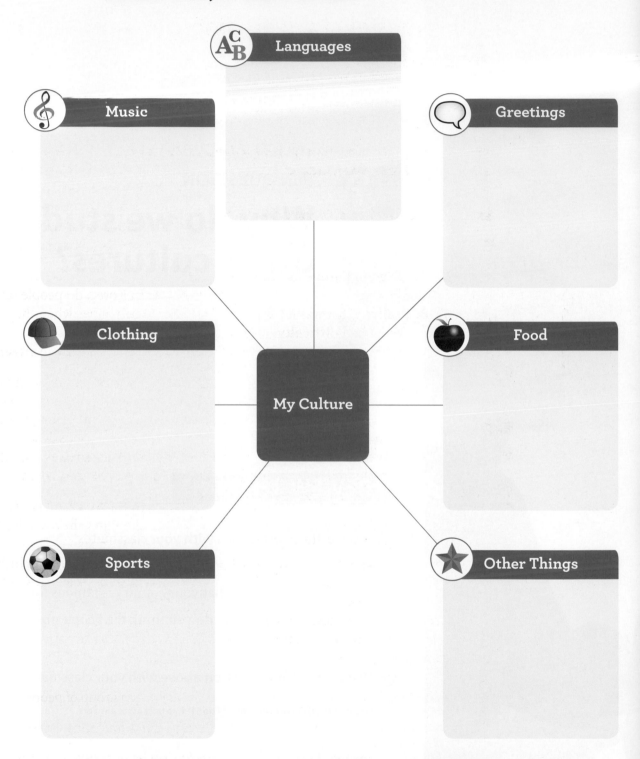

Languages

Music

Greetings

Clothing

Food

My Culture

Sports

Other Things

D Work in a group. Use your chart from Activity C and present one interesting fact about your culture to your group.

LISTENING 1 | International Advertising

VOCABULARY

Here are some words from Listening 1. Read the conversations. Match each bold word with the correct definition.

____ 1. A: I started a job at a great company.
B: Oh, where is it?
A: Well, it's an **international** company. They have offices around the world.

____ 2. A: I lived in Europe for six months.
B: Really? What was it like?
A: Well, I had **difficulty** understanding the culture, but I really enjoyed it.

____ 3. A: I made a big **mistake** at work.
B: Oh, no. What did you do?
A: I called my new boss by his first name. He looked very angry.

____ 4. A: Do colors have different meanings in different cultures?
B: Yes. Sometimes a color has a good or **positive** meaning in one culture and a bad meaning in another culture.

____ 5. A: There are different ideas around the world about **death**.
B: What do you mean?
A: I mean, in some countries people wear black and are very sad, but in others people have a party.

____ 6. A: In Korea, do people take off their shoes when they enter their homes?
B: Yes, it's a Korean **custom**.

____ 7. A: I'm going to India on business. Do you have any travel advice?
B: Yes. **Avoid** using your left hand. For example, it's very impolite to shake hands or eat with your left hand.

____ 8. A: In the Middle East, you shouldn't show the **bottom** of your shoes.
B: Why not?
A: Shoes are dirty. It's not polite.

Tip for Success

Form a "study group" with some classmates to discuss things you learn in class.

a. when a life finishes

b. a problem

c. to try not to do something

d. something that you do that is wrong

e. something a group of people usually do

f. between different countries

g. the lowest part of something

h. thinking or talking about the good parts of a situation

PREVIEW LISTENING 1

International Advertising

You are going to listen to a university business class. The professor is giving a lecture about international advertising and the problems companies have when advertising in different countries. Check (✓) the problems you think advertisers have.

- ☐ language mistakes
- ☐ problems with colors
- ☐ problems with numbers
- ☐ problems with different customs

LISTEN FOR MAIN IDEAS

 CD 1 Track 25

Read the statements. Then listen to the lecture and check (✓) the main ideas.

- ☐ a. Language differences can be a problem in international advertising.
- ☐ b. Many companies advertise their products in English.
- ☐ c. Some colors are not good to use in advertisements.
- ☐ d. Companies don't make advertising mistakes.
- ☐ e. Companies should learn about the customs of other countries.
- ☐ f. Numbers can cause problems in advertising.

LISTEN FOR DETAILS

CD 1 Track 26

The professor gives two examples of advertising mistakes. Read the information in the chart. Then listen again and check (✓) the correct information.

	Type of company	Where the mistake happened	Mistake
Example 1	☐ a computer company	☐ Eastern Europe	☐ The product smells like chicken.
	☐ a clothing company	☐ the Middle East	☐ The product name means *chicken*.
Example 2	☐ a shoe company	☐ the Middle East	☐ The advertisement showed the bottom of a man's shoes.
	☐ a telephone company	☐ Asia	☐ The advertisement showed a man with no shoes.

 **WHAT DO YOU THINK**

Discuss the questions in a group.

1. What do companies need to think about when they advertise in other countries? Give an example from your experience. Think about the problems with language, color, and customs in Listening 1.

2. What colors have special meaning in your country?

Listening Skill	Taking notes in a T-chart

 for Success

To identify the main ideas, remember to listen for key words and phrases.

When you listen, you often need to **take notes**. You can use a **T-chart** to help you organize the main ideas and details. Write the main ideas on the left side and the details on the right side. Details include *examples*, *numbers*, *facts*, *names*, and *reasons*.

Lecture: International Advertising

Main ideas	Details
Language mistakes can cause problems for companies.	• Product name has funny or strange meaning in another language • Example: computer product, Vista®—means "chicken" in some eastern European languages • Different meanings in different cultures

A. Listen to the excerpt from Listening 1. Complete the missing
information in the T-chart.

Main ideas	Details
1. _____ _____ _____	• colors have different meanings • red means _____ 2. in many countries • _____ 3. usually has positive meaning, but _____ 4. doesn't. • Example: _____ 5. means death in parts of Asia.

B. Listen to another lecture. Take notes in the T-chart. Then compare
with a partner.

Main ideas	Details

LISTENING 2 | Cultural Problems

VOCABULARY

Here are some words from Listening 2. Read the definitions. Then complete each sentence below with the correct word. Change the verb form if you need to.

> **carefully** (*adverb*) a way of doing something so you don't make a mistake
>
> **confused** (*adjective*) not able to think clearly, not understanding
>
> **die** (*verb*) to stop living
>
> **invite** (*verb*) to ask someone to come to a party or to your house
>
> **offended** (*adjective*) angry or unhappy because someone does something you don't think is polite
>
> **rude** (*adjective*) not polite
>
> **upset** (*adjective*) unhappy or worried
>
> **wedding** (*noun*) a special event when two people get married

1. There's a new student from the Ukraine in our English class. Let's _____ her to our house for dinner tomorrow.

2. I saw Lisa crying after class. She looked very _____.

3. Susan was an hour late, and she didn't call. Isn't that very _____?

4. In the Middle East, you should always say *yes* when someone offers you something. If you say *no*, the person may be _____.

5. In some countries it's common to wear black when someone _____.

6. Colors are an important part of a _____. Many women wear a white dress, but in some countries, women wear red.

7. I didn't understand English well when I visited Ireland. When people spoke, I felt a little _____. But I still had a great time.

8. Watch people _____. Then you won't make a mistake.

PREVIEW LISTENING 2

Cultural Problems

You are going to listen to three people telling about cultural problems. Look at the photos. What cultural problem do you think each shows?

1

2

3

LISTEN FOR MAIN IDEAS

CD 1
Track 29

Listen to the stories. Then check (✓) the topic of each story.

1. ☐ a. choosing a gift
   ☐ b. standing close
   ☐ c. shopping

2. ☐ a. visiting a home
   ☐ b. birthday gifts
   ☐ c. giving flowers

3. ☐ a. giving business cards
   ☐ b. business meetings
   ☐ c. getting a job

LISTEN FOR DETAILS

CD 1
Track 30

Read the statements. Then listen again. Write *T* (true) or *F* (false).

____ 1. João knew the woman in the bookstore.

____ 2. It's OK to stand very close to other people in the United States.

____ 3. Russians usually give one, three, or five flowers.

____ 4. Tanya was offended by the gift from her co-workers.

____ 5. Rick didn't bring business cards to the wedding.

____ 6. In the U.S., it's OK to take a business card with one hand.

 **WHAT DO YOU THINK?**

A. Discuss the questions in a group.

1. Do you know any of the customs from Listening 2? Read the statement and check (✓) *yes* or *no*. Then discuss your answers.

	Yes	No
1. In my culture, it's rude to stand very close to someone.	☐	☐
2. Some numbers in my culture have a special meaning.	☐	☐
3. In my culture, people only use business cards in business situations.	☐	☐

2. Do you have an example of a cultural problem? Tell your classmates the story.

B. Think about both Listening 1 and Listening 2 as you discuss the questions.

1. What problems can happen when people don't know about another culture?

2. What are some important things people from other cultures should know about your culture?

Vocabulary Skill | **Words in context**

When you listen, you will sometimes hear words you don't know. You can use other information to help you guess the meaning of new words. This is called **context**. The words that come before and after another word are the context.

> Then she looked very upset and said, "Excuse me!" and moved away.
> I didn't know what was wrong. I felt **confused**. I learned later that...

You can guess the meaning of *confused* from the context. The speaker says, "I didn't know what was wrong." *Confused* is a feeling. (The speaker says "I <u>felt</u> *confused*.") You can guess that *confused* is a feeling that you have when you don't understand.

A. Listen to a student's story about living in Australia. Use the context to guess the meaning. Circle the correct meaning of each word.

1. **depressed**
   a. very sad
   b. very offended

2. **tough**
   a. enjoyable, fun
   b. difficult or challenging

3. **considerate**
   a. caring, thoughtful
   b. rude and unkind

4. **treated**
   a. avoided
   b. behaved towards

5. **optimistic**
   a. cheerful, positive
   b. stressful and worried

CD 1
Track 32 **B.** Listen again. Write any words or phrases that helped you get the meaning. Compare your answers with a partner.

1. first time away, missed my family

2. _____

3. _____

4. _____

5. _____

SPEAKING

Grammar   Part 1   *Should* and *shouldn't*

Should and *shouldn't*

To form a sentence, use a subject + *should/shouldn't* + the base form of a verb.

> I
> You
> He / She   **should** learn customs of other countries.
> We   **shouldn't** make too many cultural mistakes.
> You
> They

Note: *Shouldn't* is the contraction for *should + not*.

Use *should* to say that it is good to do something.

> In Japan, you **should** take a business card with two hands.

When something is <u>not</u> good to do, we use *shouldn't*.

> You **shouldn't** give six or eight flowers in Russia.

 CD 1
Track 33

**A. What do you know about customs from around the world? Circle
should or *shouldn't*. Then listen and check your answers.**

1. In India, you (should / shouldn't) use your left hand to eat.

2. In Thailand, you (should / shouldn't) touch a person on the head.

3. In the U.S., you (should / shouldn't) look at people's eyes when you
   speak to them.

4. In France, when you visit someone's home, you (should / shouldn't)
   bring a gift.

5. In Saudi Arabia, you (should / shouldn't) say *no* when someone offers
   you something to eat or drink.

6. In Colombia, you (should / shouldn't) avoid giving marigolds—a yellow
   flower—as a gift.

B. What are things you should or shouldn't do in your culture? Write two sentences with *should* and two sentences with *shouldn't*. Then read your sentences to your partner.

1. _____

2. _____

3. _____

4. _____

| Grammar | *Part 2* It's + adjective + infinitive | web |

It's + (*not*) adjective + infinitive

You can make statements with *It's* + (*not*) **adjective** + **infinitive** to talk about behavior and customs. The infinitive is *to* + **the base form of a verb.**

> **It's polite to say** "thank you."
> **It's rude to show** the bottom of your feet.
> **It's common to wear** a white wedding dress.
> **It's not common to wear** a green wedding dress.
> **It's OK to use** your first name.
> **It's not OK to use** your nickname.

Note: *It's* is the contraction of *it* + *is.*

CD 1
Track 34

A. Listen to the excerpts from Listening 2. Complete the missing information.

1. There was another student standing in front of the shelf. I stood next to her and started to look for my book. Then she looked very upset and said, "Excuse me!" and moved away. I didn't know what was wrong. I was confused. I learned later that you shouldn't stand very close to other people in the U.S. _____.

2. They gave me some very nice gifts...and they gave me flowers—six flowers. In Russia, _____ of flowers, for example, one, three, five... But you shouldn't give two, four, or six flowers. We only do that when a person dies.

3. I was a little surprised. In the U.S., we only use cards for business, so I didn't bring mine. I just took the Japanese people's business cards and put them in my pocket. After the wedding, I learned that _____. You should always take the cards with two hands and read them carefully. I only used one hand, and I didn't read them at all.

B. What are customs in your culture or another culture you know? Write one sentence for each topic in the box. Use *It's* + (*not*) adjective + infinitive.

eating/drinking	greetings	visiting someone's home
gestures	holidays	workplace/office

1. _____

2. _____

3. _____

4. _____

5. _____

6. _____

C. Work in a group. Take turns reading your sentences. Ask questions if you don't understand.

Pronunciation **The schwa /ə/ sound**

CD 1
Track 35

The schwa /ə/ is the most common vowel sound in English. It sounds like the *a* in *about* /əˈbaʊt/. We pronounce the vowel in many unstressed syllables (or parts of words) with the schwa /ə/ sound. The schwa /ə/ is never in a stressed syllable.

In these examples, the vowels in red are pronounced with a schwa /ə/ sound.

avoid   cultural   custom   international   problem

CD 1
Track 36

A. Listen and repeat these words. Then <u>underline</u> the schwa sound in each word.

1. <u>a</u>void

2. bottom

3. considerate

4. mistake

5. personality

6. positive

7. similar

8. telephone

B. Write four sentences. In each sentence, use a word from Activity A. Then take turns reading your sentences with a partner.

1. _____

2. _____

3. _____

4. _____

| Speaking Skill | Presenting information from notes | |

When you present information to an audience, you should not read directly from your notes. It's important to look up and make eye contact with the audience. This makes the presentation more interesting.

Preparation

- Use small cards.
- Write only key words and phrases. Don't write the whole presentation.
- Practice your presentation.

Presentation

- Look at the audience. Then begin speaking.
- Look down briefly to check your notes.
- Make eye contact with individual people in your audience as you speak.

A. Read the Web page with tips for visiting Egypt. Underline the key words and phrases for each tip.

EGYPT
EXPLORE. DISCOVER. EXPERIENCE.

| Experience Egypt | **Culture Tips for Travelers** | Sights and Activities | Organize your trip | 🔍 |

Culture Tips for Travelers

EATING
▲ You should only use your right hand for eating. It's impolite to use the left hand. Your host may be offended.
▲ When you finish eating, your host will offer more food. Even if you are not hungry, you should take a little more. It's important to show that you enjoy the meal.

VISITING SOMEONE'S HOME
▲ You should always dress neatly and conservatively when you visit someone's home.
▲ It's common to bring a gift for the host. You should bring chocolates or other sweets. It isn't good to bring flowers because it's common to bring flowers when someone is sick.

GIFT-GIVING
▲ You should receive a gift with the right hand or both hands. You shouldn't use the left hand.
▲ You shouldn't open the gift when someone gives it to you. It's polite to wait until later.

Some Useful Words
▶ Hello
▶ How are you?
▶ Can you help me?

Getting Directions

Getting Around

Shopping

Flowers of Egypt

B. Complete the notes with the key words and phrases from the Web page.

Culture Tips for Visiting Egypt Presentation Notes

1. _____ <u>Eating</u> _____

   • only use _____ <u>your right hand</u> _____

   • impolite to use _____

   • host will _____ _____,

     you should _____

2. _____ someone's home

   • _____ and conservatively

   • bring _____,

     such as _____

   • do NOT bring _____

3. _____

   • receive a gift _____

   • do NOT use _____

   • should wait to _____

 for Success

Before you give a presentation, practice it several times. Try standing in front of a mirror. Practice speaking from notes and making eye contact until you feel comfortable.

C. Work with a partner. Take turns presenting the information. Use the information in Activity B. Be sure to look at your partner when you speak.

Unit Assignment   **Give a presentation**

Q In this assignment, you will plan and give a presentation about your culture or another culture you know well. As you prepare your presentation, think about the Unit Question, "Why do we study other cultures?" and refer to the Self-Assessment checklist on page 62.

For alternative unit assignments, see the *Q: Skills for Success Teacher's Handbook.*

CONSIDER THE IDEAS

Look again at the Web page on page 59. Discuss the questions in a group.

1. Are any of the customs in Egypt similar to customs you know? Which ones?

2. Do you think it's important to learn the customs of a country you visit? Why or why not?

PREPARE AND SPEAK

A. GATHER IDEAS Choose <u>three</u> topics in the box and write them in the chart below. Complete the chart with notes about customs in your culture or another culture you know well.

Gift-giving	Business	Gestures
Eating and drinking	Greetings	Visiting someone's home

Topic	Customs

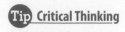

B. ORGANIZE IDEAS Use your notes from the chart in Activity A to prepare a short presentation about customs in your culture or a culture you know well. Write your presentation notes on note cards.

C. SPEAK Give your presentation to the class or to a group. Refer to the Self-Assessment checklist below before you begin. Use note cards during the presentation, and remember to look at your audience.

CHECK AND REFLECT

A. CHECK Think about the Unit Assignment as you complete the Self-Assessment checklist.

SELF-ASSESSMENT		
Yes	**No**	
☐	☐	I was able to speak easily about the topic.
☐	☐	My partner/group/class understood me.
☐	☐	I used *should/shouldn't* and *it's* + (*not*) adjective + infinitive correctly.
☐	☐	I used vocabulary from the unit.
☐	☐	I presented information from notes.
☐	☐	I correctly pronounced any words with schwa /ə/.

B. REFLECT Discuss these questions with a partner.

What is something new you learned in this unit?

 Think about the Unit Question, "Why do we study other cultures?" Do you have more answers now than when you started this unit? If yes, what new answers do you have?

Track Your Success

Circle the words you learned in this unit.

Nouns	Verbs	offended
bottom 🔑	avoid 🔑	positive 🔑 AWL
custom 🔑	die 🔑	rude 🔑
death 🔑	invite 🔑	upset 🔑
difficulty 🔑		
mistake 🔑	**Adjectives**	**Adverb**
wedding 🔑	confused 🔑	carefully 🔑
	international 🔑	

🔑 Oxford 2000 keywords
AWL Academic Word List

Check (✓) the skills you learned. If you need more work on a skill, refer to the page(s) in parentheses.

LISTENING	●	I can take notes in a T-chart. (p. 49)
VOCABULARY	●	I can guess meaning from context. (p. 53)
GRAMMAR	●	I can understand and use *should/shouldn't* and *It's* + (*not*) adjective + infinitive. (pp. 55–56)
PRONUNCIATION	●	I can recognize and pronounce the schwa /ə/ sound. (p. 57)
SPEAKING	●	I can present information from notes. (p. 58)
LEARNING OUTCOME	●	I can give a presentation about customs in a culture I know well.

UNIT 4

Positive Thinking

LISTENING ● using information questions to understand a story
VOCABULARY ● using the dictionary
GRAMMAR ● *because* and *so*
PRONUNCIATION ● syllables and syllable stress
SPEAKING ● responding in a conversation

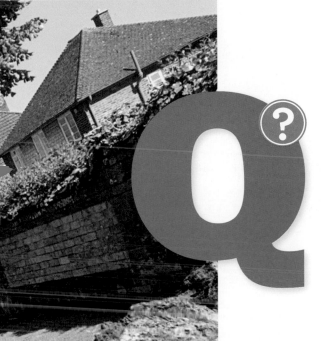

LEARNING OUTCOME ●

Participate in a group
discussion about bad
situations with
happy endings.

Q

Unit QUESTION

What makes a
happy ending?

PREVIEW THE UNIT

A **Discuss these questions with your classmates.**

Do you like happy endings in movies? Why or why not?

Can a happy ending come from something bad?

Look at the photo. Do you think it shows a happy ending?
Why or why not?

B **Discuss the Unit Question above with your classmates.**

🔊 Listen to *The Q Classroom*, Track 37 on CD 1, to hear other answers.

C Work with a partner. What stories do you know with happy endings? Make a list. Then compare your answers in groups.

STORY	HAPPY ENDING
Cinderella	Cinderella marries the prince.

D Read the statements in the chart. Which situations do you think have happy endings? Check (✓) *Happy, Unhappy,* or *Not sure.*

Situation	Happy	Unhappy	Not sure
1. Paul studied really hard for his science test.	☐	☐	☐
2. Anna didn't hear her alarm clock this morning.	☐	☐	☐
3. We want to go on a picnic today, but it's raining outside.	☐	☐	☐
4. Phil heard a loud noise in the middle of the night.	☐	☐	☐
5. I got an email from my best friend. She got a new job.	☐	☐	☐
6. Maggie has to read her report out loud to the class.	☐	☐	☐

E Compare your answers with your group. For each situation, what do you think happens next?

LISTENING 1 | A Bad Situation with a Happy Ending

VOCABULARY

(Tip) for Success

Remember to look at the context in a sentence to help you decide on the correct word to complete the sentence.

Here are some words from Listening 1. Read the definitions. Then complete each sentence with the correct word.

alive (*adjective*) living, not dead

amazing (*adjective*) surprising, difficult to believe

camp (*noun*) a place where people live in tents for a short time

distance (*noun*) how far it is from one place to another

effect (*noun*) a change that happens because of something else

hole (*noun*) an empty space or opening in something

painful (*adjective*) causing pain

suddenly (*adverb*) quickly and unexpectedly

1. It was getting dark, so the hikers went back to their _____ for the night.

2. Unusual weather is one _____ of global warming.

3. Is the _____ from your house to the airport long?

4. _____ , there was a loud noise, and everyone started to run.

5. Watch out! There's a big _____ in the road. Don't hit it with your bicycle.

6. I can't believe you won the race! That's _____.

7. Are your grandparents still _____?

8. Karen had a very _____ headache, so she went to the hospital.

Joe Simpson

PREVIEW LISTENING 1

A Bad Situation with a Happy Ending

You are going to listen to the amazing true story of mountain climber Joe Simpson. Read the title of the story. What do you think happened to Joe Simpson? Check (✓) your guess.

☐ He got lost in the mountains and never returned.

☐ He climbed a mountain faster than any other climber.

☐ He fell and broke his leg but was able to return to camp.

LISTEN FOR MAIN IDEAS

CD 1
Track 38

A. Read the sentence parts. Then listen and match the two halves of each sentence to form the story.

Siula Grande, Peru

_d_ 1. Joe and Simon   a. off the side of the mountain.

___ 2. On the way down, Joe fell and   b. Joe found a way to get through the ice.

___ 3. Simon lowered Joe down   c. a few hours before Simon planned to leave.

___ 4. Suddenly, Joe fell   d. climbed to the top of a mountain.

___ 5. Simon cut the rope and   e. Joe fell into a deep ice hole.

___ 6. After three days,   f. broke his leg.

___ 7. Joe arrived at the camp   g. the mountain with a long rope.

B. Read the story with a partner.

LISTEN FOR DETAILS

CD 1
Track 39

Read the statements. Then listen again. Write _T_ (true) or _F_ (false).

___ 1. Joe Simpson is from the United States.

___ 2. Joe Simpson and Simon Yates were mountain climbers.

___ 3. Simpson broke his leg near the top of the mountain.

___ 4. Yates saw Simpson fall off the side of the mountain.

_____ 5. Simon Yates cut the rope.

_____ 6. Joe Simpson had enough food and water for three days.

_____ 7. When Simpson came out of the ice, he was far from the camp.

_____ 8. Yates was at the camp when Simpson arrived.

Q WHAT DO YOU THINK?

Discuss the questions in a group.

1. What were the bad events in the story? What events made it have a happy ending?

2. Why did Simon Yates cut the rope? Do you think it was the right choice or the wrong choice?

| Listening Skill | Using information questions to understand a story | web+ |

When you listen to a story, you can use **information questions** to guide your listening and help you understand better. When you listen to a speaker tell a story, think about these questions:

- **Who is the story about?** Listen for people's names and personal information.
- **What happened?** Listen for actions and events.
- **When did the story happen?** Listen for dates and time expressions.
- **Where was it?** Listen for places and descriptions of places.

CD 1
Track 40   **A. Listen to Listening 1 again and write the answers to the questions.**

1. Who is the story about? _____

_____

2. What happened? _____

_____

3. When did the story happen? _____

_____

4. Where did it happen? _____

_____

CD 1
Track 41

B. Read the questions. Then listen to the news story. Take notes in your notebook. Then answer the questions with a partner.

1. Who is the story about?

2. What happened?

3. When did the story happen?

4. Where was it?

kangaroo

LISTENING 2 | Make Your Own Happy Ending

VOCABULARY

Here are some words from Listening 2. Read the sentences. Then write each bold word next to the correct definition.

1. Oh, no! My mother's birthday was yesterday, and I **completely** forgot.

2. I feel so lucky to be alive. I always want to **remember** what happened.

3. Diana had an **accident**. She fell down and broke her arm.

4. Get down from there! You should be more careful. You're going to **get hurt** someday.

5. Mr. Clark is an **expert** on mountain climbing. He wrote a book about his experience.

6. Gina has a great **attitude** about life. She doesn't worry about anything.

7. Thank you very much. I really **appreciate** all of your help.

8. I can't tell you where I'm going. It's a **secret**.

a. _____ (*noun*) the way you think or feel about something

b. _____ (*noun*) something you must not tell people

c. _____ (*noun*) something bad that happens by chance

d. _____ (*verb*) to be thankful for something

e. _____ (*noun*) a person who knows a lot about something

f. _____ (*adverb*) totally

g. _____ (*phrasal verb*) feel pain in a part of the body

h. _____ (*verb*) to keep something in your mind or bring something back into your mind

PREVIEW LISTENING 2

| Make Your Own Happy Ending

You are going to listen to a radio interview with Ellen Sharpe, the author of *Make Your Own Happy Ending*. What advice do you think she is going to give people about how to be happy? Check (✓) your guess.

☐ Appreciate the positive things in your life.

☐ Have more fun and buy lots of things.

LISTEN FOR MAIN IDEAS

CD 1
Track 42

Read the statements. Then listen and circle the main idea.

1. The book gives people a secret for how to be happy.

2. The book says that it's important to appreciate the positive things in life.

3. The book teaches people how to avoid accidents.

4. The book tells stories about happy people.

LISTEN FOR DETAILS

CD 1
Track 43

Read the questions. Then listen to the interview again. Circle the correct answer for each question.

Tip for Success

Information questions appear on many tests. The *Wh-* word at the beginning of a question will tell you what kind of information to listen for.

1. When did Ellen Sharpe's accident happen?
   a. At five years old
   b. About five years ago
   c. About five months ago

2. Why did the accident happen?
   a. Sharpe was looking for her cell phone in the car.
   b. Sharpe's boss called to ask why she was late.
   c. Another driver was driving too fast.

3. Who came to the hospital every day?
   a. Sharpe's mother and her brother
   b. Sharpe's parents and her friends
   c. Sharpe's parents and her brother

4. What happened to Sharpe after the accident?
   a. She got a good job.
   b. She had a lot of friends.
   c. She changed her attitude.

WHAT DO YOU THINK?

A. Discuss the questions in a group.

1. Think about an experience that made you feel really happy. What happened?

2. The message of Sharpe's book is to appreciate the positive things in your life. What are some things you appreciate in your life?

B. Think about Listening 1 and Listening 2 as you discuss the questions.

1. Have any of your life experiences changed your attitude about the things that are important in life? In what ways?

2. How is Ellen Sharpe's story similar to Simpson and Yates's story?

| Vocabulary Skill | Using the dictionary | |

Often, several **related words** are formed from the same root. The root word *effect,* for example, has three related words.

Look at the dictionary entry for *effective*. The related words are highlighted in yellow.

> **ef·fec·tive** /ɪˈfɛktɪv/ *adjective*
> Something that is **effective** works well: *Jogging is an effective way to stay in shape.* ⊃ **ANTONYM ineffective**
> ▸ **ef·fec·tive·ly** /ɪˈfɛktɪvli/ *adverb*: *She dealt with the situation effectively.*

Related words are often different parts of speech (*noun, verb,...*) from the root word. Sometimes they have opposite meanings (*effective, ineffective*). Learning the words related to a root word is a good way to expand your vocabulary.

All dictionary entries are from the *Oxford Basic American Dictionary for learners of English* © Oxford University Press 2011.

A. Look up each word in the dictionary. Complete the chart with the missing word forms. There may be more than one word possible in a space.

Nouns	Verbs	Adjectives	Adverbs
1. effect		effective, ineffective	effectively
2.		amazing	
3. organization		organized	
4.		confused, confusing	
5. decision		decisive	
6. accident			
7.		happy,	
8.		painful	
9.			suddenly

B. Circle the correct form of the word to complete each sentence.

1. What do you think makes you a (happy / happily) person?

2. Joe Simpson fell a long way, but (amazing / amazingly), he didn't die.

3. If you see a bear, don't make any (sudden / suddenly) moves. Just walk away very slowly.

4. Be very careful when you are cooking. You can get a (painful / painfully) burn.

5. This medicine is very (effect / effective) for headaches.

6. It is important to (organization / organize) your ideas before your presentation.

7. You shouldn't make a big (decide / decision) after a serious accident. You should wait a while.

8. I (accidental / accidentally) left my wallet at home.

Grammar *because* and *so*

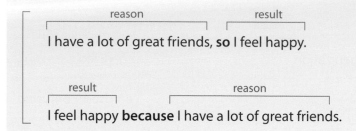

Use *because* and *so* to connect a reason with a result — that is, to give the reason for a situation or an event.

> reason | result
> I have a lot of great friends, **so** I feel happy.
>
> result | reason
> I feel happy **because** I have a lot of great friends.

A. Match the two parts of each sentence.

Tip Critical Thinking

In Activities A and B, you need to **distinguish** between the words *because* and *so*. **Distinguishing** means you look at the differences between things. This can help you understand the two things better.

 _c_ 1. Some people don't   a. so she has a lot of friends.
     eat chocolate

 ___ 2. Paula is a nice person,   b. because he always works hard.

 ___ 3. Our teacher was sick,   c̶. because they think it's bad for you.

 ___ 4. Steve has a good job   d. so we didn't have the test.

 ___ 5. It's raining,   e. because she has to work.

 ___ 6. Kim can't go shopping   f. so we can't go to the beach.

 CD 1
Track 44

B. Complete the conversations with *because* or *so*. Then listen and check your answers.

1. **A:** Why weren't you in class this morning?

 B: Well, I woke up late, _____

 I missed the train. Then I had to go back home

 _____ I forgot all my books!

 A: That's terrible.

2. **A:** My little brother is a really good student.

   B: Why do you say that?

   A: Well, he's really smart, _____
   he always gets good grades.

   B: Hmm. Maybe he gets good grades
   _____ he studies hard.

3. **A:** Hi, Joe. How was your vacation?

   B: Not very good.

   A: Oh, no. Why not?

   B: Our flight was late _____ there
   was a big storm. Then our hotel was full,
   _____ we didn't have a place to sleep.

   A: Wow! I'm sorry to hear that.

C. Take turns reading the conversations in Activity B with a partner.

Pronunciation	Syllables and syllable stress

Syllables

Words are made up of parts called **syllables**. Each syllable has a vowel sound. *Pain* has one syllable and *pain • ful* has two syllables, for example. The dictionary divides words into syllables as in the chart.

 CD 1 Track 45

Listen to these examples and count the syllables.

one syllable	two syllables	three syllables	four syllables
pain	pain • ful	a • ma •zing	ap • pre • ci • ate
camp	se • cret	com • plete • ly	ef • fec • tive • ly

Syllable stress

In words with more than one syllable, one syllable has more stress. We say the stressed syllable a little more strongly and loudly.

 CD 1 Track 46

Listen to each word. Notice the stressed syllable.

    PAIN • ful   a • MA • zing   ap • PRE • ci • ate

CD 1 Track 47

A. Listen and repeat these words. Then write the number of syllables in each word.

1. alive _2_
2. amazingly ___
3. distance __
4. effective ___

5. hurt ___
6. happily ___
7. remember ___
8. suddenly ___

CD 1 Track 48

B. Listen and circle the stressed syllable in each word. Then say the words.

1. hos • pit • al
2. com • plete • ly
3. se • cret
4. ef • fec • tive • ly

5. sud • den • ly
6. at • ti • tude
7. con • trol
8. un • hap • py

Speaking Skill | **Responding in a conversation**

In a conversation, it's important to show that you are listening and interested in what the other speaker says. This is part of participating in a conversation.

Look at these expressions:

- To show you are listening: Uh-huh. / Mm hmm. / I see.
- To show interest: Really? / Wow! / That's interesting.
- To respond to bad news: Oh, no! How awful! / That's too bad. /
  I'm sorry to hear that.
- To respond to good news: Congratulations! / That's great! /
  I'm so happy for you!

A. Listen to the excerpts from Listening 2. Complete them with expressions from the Speaking Skill box.

Ellen Sharpe: I saw people who had a lot of things, and I thought they were happy. I didn't appreciate my life.

Interviewer: _____. So, how did you become an
1.
expert on happiness?

Ellen Sharpe: Well, about five years ago, something happened that completely changed me.

Interviewer: _____ _____ __? What happened?
2.

Ellen Sharpe: I don't remember everything, but I woke up in the hospital.

Interviewer: _____.
3.

Ellen Sharpe: My parents and my brother came to visit me every day. Every time I saw them, I felt happy. They were all there when I really needed them.

Interviewer: _____! It sounds like this experience really
4.
changed your attitude.

Ellen Sharpe: That's what the book is about. I want to help other people be happy, too.

Interviewer: _____. That's great advice, Ellen.
5.

B. With a partner, practice reading the conversation in Activity A.

Remember to ask
for repetition if you
don't understand
something, and ask
follow-up questions
if you want more
information.

C. Take turns asking and answering these questions with your partner. Use the expressions from the Speaking Skill box on page 76 to respond to your partner.

1. Do you think you are a happy person? Why or why not?

2. What do you appreciate most about your life?

3. Tell about a time when you had a happy ending to a bad situation.

Unit Assignment | **Have a group discussion**

 In this assignment, you will have a group discussion about bad situations with happy endings. As you prepare to speak, think about the Unit Question, "What makes a happy ending?" and refer to the Self-Assessment checklist on page 80.

For alternative unit assignments, see the *Q: Skills for Success Teacher's Handbook*.

CONSIDER THE IDEAS

CD 1
Track 50

Listen to Yuko and Diego talk about bad situations with happy endings. Check (✓) the correct information for each person.

Person	Bad situation	Happy ending
Yuko	1. ☐ She was a flight attendant and there was a plane accident. ☐ She missed an interview because she got hurt.	2. ☐ She decided to become a nurse. ☐ She was in the hospital for a month and got better.
Diego	3. ☐ He failed a test. ☐ He failed math class.	4. ☐ He studied hard and became a math tutor. ☐ He got into a good university and found a job he likes.

PREPARE AND SPEAK

A. GATHER IDEAS Think about three bad situations that had happy endings. They can be about you or someone you know. Make notes in the chart.

Bad situation	Happy ending

B. ORGANIZE IDEAS Complete these tasks as you prepare for your group discussion.

1. Choose one of the situations from your chart in Activity A to talk about with your group.

2. Write sentences to explain the bad situation and its happy ending.

   I was unhappy because…   …so it had a happy ending.

C. SPEAK Have a group discussion about bad situations with happy endings. Refer to the Self-Assessment checklist on page 80 before you begin.

CHECK AND REFLECT

A. CHECK Think about the Unit Assignment as you complete the Self-Assessment checklist.

Yes	No	SELF-ASSESSMENT
☐	☐	I was able to speak easily about the topic.
☐	☐	My partner/group/class understood me.
☐	☐	I used *because* and *so* correctly.
☐	☐	I used vocabulary from the unit.
☐	☐	I responded in conversations.
☐	☐	I stressed words correctly.

B. REFLECT Discuss these questions with a partner.

What is something new you learned in this unit?

 Look back at the Unit Question, "What makes a happy ending?" Is your answer different now than when you started this unit? If yes, how is it different? Why?

Track Your Success

Circle the words you learned in this unit.

Nouns
accident 🔑
attitude 🔑 AWL
camp 🔑
distance 🔑
effect 🔑
expert 🔑 AWL
hole 🔑
secret 🔑

Verbs
appreciate 🔑 AWL
remember

Adjectives
alive 🔑
amazing
painful 🔑

Adverbs
completely 🔑
suddenly 🔑

Phrase
get hurt

Expressions
I see.
Mm hmm.
Uh-huh.
Really?
Wow!
That's great.
That's interesting.
I'm sorry to hear that.
Oh, no! That's too bad.

🔑 Oxford 2000 keywords
AWL Academic Word List

Check (✓) the skills you learned. If you need more work on a skill, refer to the page(s) in parentheses.

LISTENING ●	I can use information questions to understand a story. (p. 69)
VOCABULARY ●	I can find related words in the dictionary. (p. 72)
GRAMMAR ●	I can use *because* and *so*. (p. 74)
PRONUNCIATION ●	I can recognize syllables and syllable stress. (p. 75)
SPEAKING ●	I can respond in a conversation. (p. 76)
LEARNING OUTCOME ●	I can participate in a group discussion about bad situations with happy endings.

UNIT 5

Vacation Time

LISTENING	●	understanding numbers and dates
VOCABULARY	●	suffixes *-ful* and *-ing*
GRAMMAR	●	*be going to*
PRONUNCIATION	●	reduction of *be going to*
SPEAKING	●	introducing topics in a presentation

Give a presentation describing a tour to a popular travel destination.

Unit QUESTION

What is the best kind of vacation?

PREVIEW THE UNIT

A **Discuss these questions with your classmates.**

What did you do on your last vacation?

What are popular places for tourists in your home country?

Look at the photo. Would you enjoy this kind of vacation? Why or why not?

B **Discuss the Unit Question above with your classmates.**

))) Listen to *The Q Classroom*, **Track 2 on CD 2,** to hear other answers.

C Work with a partner. Look at the signs and complete the information below.

1.

location of signs:

_____

meaning of signs:

_____

_____

2.

location of signs:

_____

meaning of signs:

_____

_____

3.

location of signs:

_____

meaning of signs:

_____

_____

D Look again at the signs in Activity C. In a group, discuss these questions.

1. Why do you think the signs were put up?

2. Do you think people need signs like these?

3. Do you have examples of interesting or funny signs? Draw or explain one to your group.

LISTENING 1 | Places in Danger

VOCABULARY

Here are some words from Listening 1. Read the definitions. Then complete each sentence with the correct word.

 for Success

Pay attention to the Listening title. Think about it before you start listening. Ask yourself, *What is this about? What do I know about this topic?*

> **dangerous** (*adjective*) may hurt you
>
> **destroy** (*verb*) to break or ruin something
>
> **electric** (*adjective*) using power that comes through wires
>
> **insect** (*noun*) a small animal with six legs, such as an ant or a fly
>
> **local** (*adjective*) of a place near you
>
> **pollution** (*noun*) dirty air or water
>
> **shake** (*verb*) to move quickly up and down or from side to side
>
> **tourist** (*noun*) a person who visits a place on vacation

1. If you travel to Mexico, you should try the _____ _____ food. Tacos are my favorite dish.

2. Suddenly, the building started to _____ . We all ran outside.

3. Too many visitors could _____ these very old houses.

4. Many big cities have problems with _____. Cars and buses make the air dirty.

5. Many countries need _____ _____ to help the local economy.

6. Do you think it's _____ to travel alone?

7. What kind of _____ is that? It's such a colorful bug.

8. Some city buses don't need to use gas. They're _____.

PREVIEW LISTENING 1

Places in Danger

You are going to listen to a podcast of a travel program called "Places in Danger." The program talks about the negative effects of tourists visiting three famous places. Why do you think they are in danger?

Look at these famous places.

Taj Mahal, India

Galapagos Islands, Ecuador

The Great Pyramid, Egypt

LISTEN FOR MAIN IDEAS

 CD 2
Track 3

Read the items. Then listen to the podcast. Circle the best answer to complete each main idea.

1. The Taj Mahal became darker because of
   a. bicycles near the building.
   b. millions of tourists walking on it.
   c. pollution from cars and buses.

2. In the Galapagos Islands, planes and boats
   a. bring insects that don't belong there.
   b. carry dangerous liquids.
   c. have a lot of accidents.

3. The Great Pyramid is in danger because
   a. it's made of many stones.
   b. cars and buses shake the ground.
   c. too many tourists walk there.

LISTEN FOR DETAILS

CD 2
Track 4

Read the sentences. Then listen again. Circle the correct information to complete each sentence.

1. The Taj Mahal was built for the (wife / daughter) of the Indian leader.

2. Only bicycles and electric (buses / cars) can go near the Taj Mahal.

3. The Galapagos Islands are home to thousands of (people / animals).

4. In the Galapagos Islands, airlines spray liquids to kill dangerous (insects / plants).

5. The Great Pyramid is fragile because of its (size / age).

6. Tourists must (drive / walk) to the Pyramid.

 WHAT DO YOU THINK?

Discuss the questions in a group.

1. Were you surprised about the problems at these places? Why or why not?

2. Think of one more idea to help each place. Then share it with the class.

3. Name some famous places in your country. Do tourists cause any problems there?

| Listening Skill | Understanding numbers and dates |

It's important to understand numbers when you listen, for example, when you listen to detailed information on a TV or radio program or during a lecture.

Numbers ending in *-teen* or *-ty* can be difficult. You need to listen carefully for the stress patterns in these numbers. That way you can be sure you understand the numbers correctly.

- **In numbers ending in *-ty*,** the first syllable is stressed: FIF-ty.
- **In numbers ending in *-teen*,** the stress is on the last syllable: fif-TEEN.

CD 2
Track 5

Listen to these pairs of numbers.

☐ 14 / 40   15 / 50   16 / 60   17 / 70   18 / 80   19 / 90

Listen to these large numbers.

453	four hundred fifty-three
3,227	three thousand two hundred twenty-seven
15,609	fifteen thousand six hundred nine
275,000	two hundred seventy-five thousand
8,250,000	eight million two hundred fifty thousand

Listen to these dates.

1700 → seventeen hundred	1989 → nineteen eighty-nine
1809 → eighteen oh nine	2011 → twenty eleven
	(two thousand eleven)

A. Listen to these excerpts from Listening 1. Circle the numbers you hear.

Tip for Success

To practice listening for numbers and dates, watch the news in English every day. If you watch videos of the news online, you can repeat them many times.

1. The Taj Mahal was built in (632 / 1632) by the leader of India. He built the amazing white building for his wife after she died. It took (2,000 / 20,000) workers and many years to finish the building. Each year, over (30,000 / 3,000,000) tourists visit this amazing white building.

2. The Galapagos Islands are in the Pacific Ocean near South America. The (19 / 90) main islands are home to thousands of plants and animals. About (17,500 / 175,000) tourists visit the islands every year.

3. The Great Pyramid is (450 / 4,500) years old. It is (137 / 1,037) meters high. Workers used over (200,000 / 2,000,000) stones to build the pyramid.

B. Complete the travel quiz with a partner. Then listen and check your answers.

What do you know about the world?
Take this travel quiz, and find out!

1. Mt. Everest is ____ meters high.
   a. 850
   b. 8,850
   c. 9,580

2. The Eiffel Tower in Paris was built in ____.
   a. 1599
   b. 1702
   c. 1889

3. Burj Khalifa, the tallest building in the world, is ____ meters tall.
   a. 818
   b. 880
   c. 8,018

4. The population of New York City is about ____.
   a. 83,000
   b. 8,300,000
   c. 63,000,000

5. Only ____ tourists are allowed inside the Great Pyramid every day.
   a. 13
   b. 30
   c. 300

6. The Colosseum in Rome, Italy was built around the year ____.
   a. A.D. 17
   b. A.D. 70
   c. A.D. 700

7. There are ____ islands in the Philippines.
   a. 717
   b. 7,107
   c. 71,000

8. Angel Falls in Venezuela is the world's tallest waterfall. It's ____ meters tall.
   a. 979
   b. 1,065
   c. 2,500

LISTENING 2 | A Helpful Vacation

VOCABULARY

Here are some words from Listening 2. Read the sentences. Circle the word or phrase that best defines each bold word.

1. After college, Yolanda wants work as a **volunteer**.
   a. someone who works without pay
   b. someone who does difficult work

2. We really enjoyed our trip to Europe. We saw lots of **pretty** towns and took some great pictures.
   a. dangerous
   b. beautiful

3. China has the largest **population** of all the world's countries.
   a. number of people
   b. number of buildings

4. The Great Pyramid is an **ancient** site. No one knows exactly how the Egyptians built it.
   a. very small
   b. very old

5. I'm going to France tomorrow, so I have to pack my bags and **prepare** for my trip.
   a. get ready
   b. get tired

6. We waited in the airport for a long time. There was a problem with the airplane and they had to **repair** it.
   a. fix
   b. destroy

7. In the summer, I work as a tour guide. I **lead** tourists to interesting places in my hometown.
   a. take
   b. shake

8. I love to travel and learn about different cultures. It's very **enjoyable**.
   a. not fun
   b. fun

PREVIEW LISTENING 2

A Helpful Vacation

Volunteer Vacations is a travel company that offers work and travel around the world. You are going to listen to the owner of the company giving a presentation about jobs for volunteers in Cusco, Peru.

Look at the pictures. Check (✓) the activities you think the volunteers will do.

1

Tourists at Machu Picchu

2

Volunteers painting a school

3

Volunteer teacher

4

Peruvian beach

LISTEN FOR MAIN IDEAS

 CD 2
Track 10

Read the items. Then listen to the information. Check (✓) the things that the volunteers are going to do.

____ a. work on a farm

____ b. visit Machu Picchu

____ c. study Spanish

____ d. visit museums

____ e. live with a host family

____ f. relax on the beach

____ g. help sick people

____ h. teach at a school

____ i. repair a school

LISTEN FOR DETAILS

CD 2
Track 11

Listen again. Circle the correct answer.

1. The population of Cusco is about _____.
   a. 35,000
   b. 350,000
   c. 3,500,000

2. Machu Picchu is _____.
   a. a pretty city
   b. not near the mountains
   c. three hours from Cusco

3. The trip starts on _____.
   a. June 13
   b. June 30
   c. July 5

4. The group is going to study Spanish for _____.
   a. two weeks
   b. three weeks
   c. four weeks

5. At the school, volunteers can _____.
   a. teach Spanish
   b. study music
   c. teach English

6. Volunteers say that teaching the children is _____.
   a. amazing
   b. enjoyable
   c. not fun

 ## WHAT DO YOU THINK?

A. Discuss the questions in a group.

1. Do you think this volunteer tour sounds like an exciting vacation? Why or why not?

2. Do you want to take a volunteer tour? Where do you want to go?

3. How can you help in another place?

B. Think about both Listening 1 and Listening 2 as you discuss the question.

1. What are some of the good and bad effects of tourists visiting famous places? Add more *good* and *bad* effects to the T-chart below.

Good	Bad
brings money to local people	causes pollution

2. What activities can volunteer tourists do to help the people in your country or where you live?

Vocabulary Skill **Suffixes -*ful* and -*ing***

> **Suffixes** are letters or groups of letters at the end of a word. Suffixes can change the tense (-*ed*, -*ing*), the number (-*s*, -*es*), or the part of speech of a word. Learning different suffixes is a good way to build your vocabulary.
>
> - The suffix -*ful* changes a noun to an adjective.
>
>   beauty → **beautiful**   The Taj Mahal is a **beautiful** white building.
>   wonder → **wonderful**   The restaurants in Bangkok are **wonderful**.
>
> - The suffix -*ing* can change a verb to an adjective.
>
>   excite → **exciting**   Tokyo is an **exciting** place. There are many fun things to do.
>   interest → **interesting**   Our visit to Machu Picchu was very **interesting**.

A. Read the sentences. Write the adjective form of each word in parentheses.

1. If you go to Peru, you should visit Machu Picchu. The old stone

   buildings are _____ (amaze).

2. Until about 1920, the Galapagos Islands were very _____

   (peace). Only animals lived there, no people.

3. Sometimes tourists can be _____ (help) to the place they

   visit. They create jobs for local people.

4. We visited Venice, Italy during our last vacation. It is a very

    _____ (charm) city.

5. I don't want to just go to the beach for my vacation. I want to do

    something _____ (meaning), like volunteer work.

6. The Great Pyramid is in danger because of the _____

    (rise) number of tourists in Egypt.

7. Did you enjoy your volunteer tour? I want to take one next year. I heard

    it's a very _____ (interest) experience.

8. Tourists can't touch anything inside the Great Pyramid. It's very fragile,

    so you have to be _____ (care).

B. Write four sentences about a tourist place you visited. Use the words
to form adjectives with *-ing* or *-ful*.

1. _____ ___

    (wonder)

2. _____

    (amaze)

3. _____

    (excite)

4. _____

    (beauty)

C. Share your sentences with a partner. Ask follow-up questions about
the vacations or places.

A: Beijing is a wonderful city.

B: Oh, when did you go there?

A: Last summer. It was hot there.

Grammar | **Be going to**

Be going to statements

We use *be going to* + base verb to talk about the future, usually about our future plans.

> Tomorrow, we**'re going to visit** the Taj Mahal.
> I**'m going to take** a volunteer tour this summer.

- To form the future with *be going to*, use *am*, *is*, or *are* + *going to* + the base form of the verb.

> She **is going to study** Spanish for two weeks.
> They **are going to repair** a school in Peru.

- To make a negative statement, use *not* before *going to*.

> I **am not going to stay** in a hotel.
> We **are not going to go** shopping today.

- In speaking and informal writing, we often use contractions

> John**'s going to fly** to the Galapagos Islands in the morning.
> The museum **isn't going to be** open tomorrow.

Be going to questions

- Form *yes/no* questions by changing the order of the subject and *be*.

> **They are going to** volunteer in Peru.
> **Are they going to** volunteer in Peru?

- Form information questions by adding the *wh-* word and changing the order of the subject and *be*.

> **Where are they going to** volunteer?

A. Read the email about a tree-planting tour in Nepal. Complete the sentences using the correct form of *be going to* and the verbs in parentheses. Use contractions.

From: jen.miller22@greatmail.com
To: ken_fujiwaka@getmail.com
Subject: Summer plans

Hi Ken,

I'm writing to tell you about my exciting summer plans. _I'm going to join_ a
1. (join)
volunteer tour to Nepal! Here are some of the things we _____.
2. (do)
On the first day we _____ a bus to Gorkha, the old capital of
3. (take)
Nepal. It _____ a long trip—five hours! I hope it doesn't rain.
4. (be)
The tour Web site says on a clear day, you can see Mt. Everest from the
bus window! We _____ three days hiking and camping in the
5. (spend)
Himalayas. Our guide _____ us about the mountain plants and
6. (teach)
animals. Then our group _____ in a small town and help the local
7. (stop)
people plant trees. I think that _____ the most enjoyable part of
8. (be)
the trip. Well, I have to go.

I _____ a blog, so you can
9. (write)
read all about the trip!

Take care,

Jen

CD 2
Track 12

B. Match the questions with the answers. Then listen to the conversations and check your answers.

____ 1. What are you going to do in China?

a. No, we're going to go shopping.

____ 2. Where are we going to stay?

b. Yes, he's going to go to Hawaii.

____ 3. Can we go to the Great Pyramid today?

c. We're going to return on May 16th.

____ 4. How long is your trip?   d. You're going to live with a local family.

____ 5. Is John going to take   e. I'm going to do volunteer work
a vacation this year?   in Shanghai.

C. Write questions. Use _be going to_. Then ask and answer the questions with a partner.

1. What / you / do this weekend

   What are you going to do this weekend _____?

2. you / study English / this weekend

   _____?

3. What / you / do / during the next holiday

   _____?

4. Where / you / travel / next summer?

   _____?

| **Pronunciation** | **Reduction of _be going to_** | |

When using **be going to**, speakers, especially in the United States, often pronounce _going to_ as _gonna_. They reduce the sounds.

CD 2
Track 13

Listen and repeat these sentences. The speaker reads them twice. Pay attention to the pronunciation of _going to_ the first time you hear each sentence, and the pronunciation of _gonna_ the second time.

1. We're going to visit Italy next year.
2. She isn't going to come with us.
3. I'm going to stay with a family in Madrid.
4. They aren't going to join a tour.

Note: We never write _gonna_ in academic or professional writing.

A. Write answers to the questions. Use *be going to*. Then take turns asking and answering the questions with a partner. Use the reduced pronunciation of *going to*.

1. A: When are you going to take your next vacation?

   B: _____.

2. A: Where are you going to go?

   B: _____.

3. A: Who are you going to travel with?

   B: _____.

4. A: What are you going to do there?

   B: _____.

B. Imagine you are going to take a volunteer tour. Use the questions in Activity A to plan your trip. Ask and answer the questions about your trip with your partner.

| Speaking Skill | Introducing topics in a presentation |

When you give a presentation, you want it to be organized so that your audience can follow what you are saying. Here are some useful expressions for organizing a presentation.

- To introduce the first topic:

  Let's start with...
  The first thing I'm going to talk about is...

- To change to a new topic:

  Now let's move on to...
  Next I'm going to explain...

- To introduce the last topic:

  Finally, let's talk about...
  To wrap up, I'll tell you about...

- To introduce the next speaker (when there is more than one):

  Now Pamela is going to tell you about...
  Now Jun Ho is going to take over.

A. Work with a partner. Imagine you work for a tour company. You are going to present the tour to a group of tourists. Decide on the best order to present these topics. Number them 1 to 6.

____ the volunteer activities

____ the cost of the trip

____ the food

____ the first day

____ the flight information

____ the schedule of places to visit

B. Take turns making sentences using the phrases in the Speaking Skill box on page 98 and the topics in Activity A. Follow the order you decided in Activity A.

The first thing I'm going to talk about is the schedule...

Unit Assignment | Plan and present a travel tour

In this assignment, you are going to work in a group to plan a vacation for tourists and then present the tour to your class. As you plan your presentation, think about the Unit Question, "What is the best kind of vacation?" and refer to the Self-Assessment checklist on page 100.

For alternative unit assignments, see the *Q: Skills for Success Teacher's Handbook*.

CONSIDER THE IDEAS

CD 2
Track 14

A. Listen to two tour guides present information about a tour to Nepal. Number the topics in order.

____ Schedule

____ Activities

____ Lodging

____ Cost

____ Food

CD 2
Track 15

B. Listen again and write notes in your notebook about the details for each topic in Activity A. Then compare your notes with a partner.

PREPARE AND SPEAK

A. **GATHER IDEAS** Work with a group. Imagine you work for a tour company.

1. Choose a travel destination and plan a tour to that place. Think of a place you know well or do some research on a new destination.

2. Make notes in your notebook, including information on schedule, lodging, food, activities, and cost.

for Success

Here are some useful phrases for adding information when your co-presenter is speaking:
May I say one more thing? / I'd like to add one point. / Can I add something?

B. **ORGANIZE IDEAS** With your group, plan a presentation to give information about your tour. Use visuals such as a poster or photos in your presentation. Decide who will talk about each topic. Use your notes from Activity A.

C. **SPEAK** Practice your presentation. Refer to the Self-Assessment checklist below before you begin. Then give your presentation to the class or to another group.

CHECK AND REFLECT

A. **CHECK** Think about the Unit Assignment as you complete the Self-Assessment checklist.

Yes	No	SELF-ASSESSMENT
☐	☐	I was able to speak easily about the topic.
☐	☐	My partner/group/class understood me.
☐	☐	I used *be going to* correctly.
☐	☐	I used vocabulary from the unit.
☐	☐	I introduced topics in a presentation.
☐	☐	I pronounced *be going to* correctly.

B. **REFLECT** Discuss these questions with a partner.

What is something new you learned in this unit?

 Think about the Unit Question, "What is the best kind of vacation?" Is your answer different now than when you started this unit? If yes, how is it different? Why?

Track Your Success

Circle the words you learned in this unit.

Nouns
insect 🔑
pollution 🔑
population
tourist 🔑
volunteer AWL

Verbs
destroy 🔑
lead 🔑
prepare 🔑
repair 🔑
shake 🔑

Adjectives
ancient 🔑
dangerous 🔑
electric 🔑
enjoyable 🔑
local 🔑
pretty 🔑

Phrases
Let's start with...
The first thing I'm going
   to talk about is...
Now let's move on to...
Now (name) is going to
   tell you about...
To wrap up, I'll tell
   you about...
Finally, let's talk
   about...

🔑 Oxford 2000 keywords
AWL Academic Word List

Check (✓) the skills you learned. If you need more work on a skill, refer to the page(s) in parentheses.

LISTENING	⬤	I can understand numbers and dates. (pp. 87–88)
VOCABULARY	⬤	I can recognize and use the suffixes -ful and -ing. (p. 93)
GRAMMAR	⬤	I can recognize and use be going to. (p. 95)
PRONUNCIATION	⬤	I can recognize and use the reduced pronunciation of be going to. (p. 97)
SPEAKING	⬤	I can introduce topics in a presentation. (p. 98)
LEARNING OUTCOME	⬤	I can give a presentation describing a tour to a popular travel destination.

UNIT

6

Laughter

LISTENING ● listening for specific information
VOCABULARY ● synonyms
GRAMMAR ● simple present for informal narratives
PRONUNCIATION ● simple present third-person -*s*/-*es*
SPEAKING ● using eye contact, pause, and tone of voice

Q

Unit QUESTION

Who makes you laugh?

PREVIEW THE UNIT

A **Discuss these questions with your classmates.**

What funny movie or TV show do you like?

Do you tell jokes or make other people laugh?

Look at the photo. Do you think it is funny?
Why or why not?

B **Discuss the Unit Question above with your classmates.**

Listen to *The Q Classroom*, **Track 16** on **CD 2**, to hear other answers.

C Look at the photo. The group is laughing at something they see on the laptop. What are possible reasons they are laughing? Write your ideas. Then discuss them with a partner.

_____

_____

_____

A: I think they are laughing at a new YouTube video.

B: I think they are looking at someone's childhood pictures.

D Look at the chart. Write your answers. Then with your partner, take turns asking for and giving information from the chart. Write your partner's answers in the chart.

Who Makes You Laugh?

Write the name of ...	You	Your partner
1. a friend who is funny		
2. a teacher who is funny		
3. someone in your family who makes you laugh		
4. someone in your class who is funny		

LISTENING

LISTENING 1 | Jackie Chan—Action-Comedy Hero

VOCABULARY

Here are some words from Listening 1. Read the sentences. Then write each bold word next to the correct definition.

1. Robin Williams, Woody Allen, and Chris Rock are all famous **comedians**.

2. Jackie Chan can jump and kick really high. He is very **powerful**.

3. My boss has a great **sense of humor**. She makes everyone laugh.

4. Angelina joined the drama club at school. She wants to be a **professional** actor someday.

5. That TV show was popular in the U.S. **However**, it was not successful in other parts of the world.

6. The movie was a big **hit**. People waited in long lines to see it in the theater.

7. We're going to see the new comedy **film** at the theater. Do you want to come?

8. The Smiths' new house is **huge**. It has ten bedrooms!

a. _____ (*noun*) movie

b. _____ (*adverb*) but

c. _____ (*adjective*) very big

d. _____ (*adjective*) doing something for money as a job

e. _____ (*noun*) people whose job is to make people laugh

f. _____ (*adjective*) having a lot of strength

g. _____ (*noun*) a person or thing that a lot of people like

h. _____ (*noun*) the ability to laugh at things and think they are funny

PREVIEW LISTENING 1

Jackie Chan—Action-Comedy Hero

You are going to listen to a radio program about Jackie Chan, a popular action-comedy film star. Look at the photos. Why do you think people will say Jackie Chan is funny? Give two reasons.

LISTEN FOR MAIN IDEAS

CD 2
Track 17

Listen and number the topics in the order the speaker talks about them. There are two topics you will not use.

 for Success

Photos can help you predict the topic and main ideas of a listening.

____ a. School days

____ b. Family

____ c. Professional acting career

____ d. University

____ e. International career

____ f. Birthplace

LISTEN FOR DETAILS

CD 2
Track 18

Listen again. Circle the correct information.

1. Jackie Chan was born in (April / August).

2. Chan's real name means "born in (Hong Kong / Beijing)."

3. In the mid-1970s, he started his (school days / acting career).

4. He became a star first in (Hollywood / Hong Kong).

5. Chan's first Hollywood films were (not popular / very popular).

6. Chan starred in *Rush Hour* in (1978 / 1998).

 **WHAT DO YOU THINK?**

Discuss the questions in a group.

1. Why do people think Jackie Chan is funny? Do you think this type of sense of humor is funny?

2. Do you like *Kung Fu* or other similar movies? Why or why not?

3. Who are famous comedy stars from your country? Why do you think they are popular?

| Listening Skill | Listening for specific information | |

> **Listening for specific information** means listening for the important details you need. We listen for specific information especially when we listen to news or weather reports, transportation schedules, and instructions. Specific information includes details such as:
>
> - names of people or places
> - numbers, dates, or times (See Unit 5 Listening Skill, pages 87–88.)
> - events

CD 2
Track 19

A. Read the information below. Then listen to Listening 1 again and write the missing information.

1. Jackie Chan's birth date: _____ _____.

2. When he moved to Hollywood: _ ____ _____.

3. What Americans thought of Chan in *Rush Hour*: _____.

4. Three reasons why he is funny:

   a. He smiles and _____.

   b. He's so _____.

   c. Fans love watching _____.

B. Listen to the end of the radio program. Write the missing information.

Chan made two more *Rush Hour* movies in _____ and

_____. He also starred with actor Owen Wilson in the
          2
comedy movies *Shanghai Noon* and *Shanghai Knights*. There are plans

for a _____ *Shanghai* movie sometime in the future, called
          3
Shanghai Dawn. In _____, Chan starred in the Hong Kong
                          4
drama *The Shinjuku Incident*. In this movie, Chan plays a more serious

character—a Chinese worker who lives in _____. Does
                                                  5
this serious role mean that Chan is giving up comedy? His fans hope

not. They think _____ is what Jackie does best.
                        6

So long for now, listeners. Tune in next week when we'll …

| Can Anyone Be Funny?

VOCABULARY

Here are some words from Listening 2. Read the sentences. Circle the best definition for each bold word.

1. Sometimes I don't **understand** jokes in English. I feel confused about what is funny.
   a. to know what something means
   b. to listen carefully to

2. Rei has a great sense of humor. She will **probably** laugh when I tell her the joke.
   a. not really
   b. almost certainly

3. Oh, no! I brought the **wrong** book to English class. This is my Spanish book.
   a. incorrect
   b. interesting

4. Do you think it's funny to **make fun of** other people?
   a. to talk quietly to
   b. to laugh at in an unkind way

5. Marisol is **afraid** to stand in front of an audience. She feels very nervous.
   a. scared
   b. happy

6. Some people don't like to show their **feelings**. They don't laugh or cry in front of other people.
   a. emotions such as happiness and anger
   b. parts of the body

7. When you give a presentation, it's important to **make eye contact** with the audience.
   a. to look in the eyes of
   b. to avoid the eyes of

8. Close your eyes and **imagine** that you are at the beach.
   a. to make a picture in your mind
   b. to draw a picture on paper

PREVIEW LISTENING 2

| Can Anyone Be Funny?

You are going to listen to a TV interview with Larry Tate, the owner of a comedy theater. In the interview, he discusses the question, "Can anyone be funny?"

What's your opinion?

☐ Anyone can be funny.   ☐ Only some people can be funny.

LISTEN FOR MAIN IDEAS

CD 2
Track 21

Read the items. Then listen to the interview. Circle the answer to complete the advice that Larry Tate gives.

1. Try to find
   a. someone who will laugh.
   b. the humor in everyday life.
   c. funny family members.

2. You shouldn't be shy about
   a. being a comedian.
   b. telling funny stories.
   c. meeting new people.

3. It's good to make fun of
   a. other people.
   b. children.
   c. yourself.

4. To be funny, people should
   a. use their voices, faces, and bodies.
   b wear funny clothes.
   c. show lots of pictures.

LISTEN FOR DETAILS

CD 2
Track 22

Read the sentences. Then listen again. Write _T_ (true) or _F_ (false).

____ 1. Tate thinks only professional comedians can be funny.

____ 2. He says it's funny to talk about situations that make you feel embarrassed.

___ 3. The joke about his son is true.

___ 4. He says that making fun of yourself helps people relax.

___ 5. The joke about his wife is true.

___ 6. He thinks it's bad to show your feelings.

 ## WHAT DO YOU THINK?

A. Discuss the questions in a group.

1. Do you agree that anyone can be funny? Why or why not?

2. Do you think Tate's advice is good? What other advice would you give to help people be funny?

3. What are favorite funny topics in your culture?

B. Think about both Listening 1 and Listening 2 as you discuss the questions.

1. How is the humor in a comedy film different than in a live theater? How are they the same?

2. Often in both movies and live comedy comedians make fun of themselves (their appearance, their culture, etc.). Do you like to laugh at yourself? Why or why not?

Vocabulary Skill   Synonyms

Synonyms are words that have almost the same or a similar meaning. The dictionary often gives synonyms in the definition of a word. In the examples, a synonym is given for *funny* while for *movie* only a definition is provided.

fun·ny /ˈfʌni/ *adjective* (fun·ni·er, fun·ni·est)
1 making you laugh or smile: *a funny story* •
He's so funny! ⊃ **SYNONYM amusing**
2 strange or surprising: *There's a funny smell in this room.*

mov·ie /ˈmuvi/ *noun*
1 [*count*] a story shown in moving pictures that you see in theaters or on television: *Would you like to **see a movie?***

You can build your vocabulary by learning synonyms for words you already know. Learning synonyms will help you understand more when you listen.

All dictionary entries are from the *Oxford Basic American Dictionary for learners of English* © Oxford University Press 2011.

A. Read the sentences. Write a synonym from the box for each underlined word. You may use some synonyms more than once. Use your dictionary to help you.

famous	funny	huge	laugh	feelings

1. Did you see the movie *King Kong*? It's about an <u>enormous</u> gorilla.

   enormous: _____

2. My friend Tomás is <u>hilarious</u>. He always makes me laugh.

   hilarious: _____

3. Jackie Chan started acting when he was eight years old. But he didn't become <u>well known</u> in the U.S. until the 1980s.

   well known: _____

4. An actor needs to be able to show different <u>emotions</u> such as anger or excitement.

   emotions: _____

5. Those two students are rude. They sit in the back of the class and <u>giggle</u>.

   giggle: _____

6. Children often make <u>silly</u> faces to make other kids laugh.

   silly: _____

B. Look in the dictionary to find one more synonym for each of these words. Write a sentence with each new synonym.

1. Word: huge   Synonym: _____

   Sentence: _____

2. Word: laugh   Synonym: _____

   Sentence: _____

3. Word: funny   Synonym: _____

   Sentence: _____

C. Work with a partner. Read your synonyms and sentences from Activity B to your partner.

| Grammar | Simple present for informal narratives | |

When you tell a short, informal narrative, like a story or a joke, you can use the simple present even if the story happened in the past.

> A man **walks** into a shop and **sees** a little rabbit. He **asks** the shopkeeper, "Does your rabbit bite?"
> The shopkeeper **says**, "No, my rabbit doesn't bite."
> The man **touches** the rabbit, and the rabbit **bites** him.
> "Ouch!" He **says**, "You said your rabbit doesn't bite!"
> The shopkeeper **replies**, "That isn't my rabbit!"

CD 2
Track 23

A. Complete these jokes with the simple present form of the verbs in the box. Then listen and check your answers.

1.

| reply | bring | go | say | order |

A man and a woman _____ _____ to a restaurant
                              1.
for lunch. The woman _____ _____ a bowl of soup.
                            2.
A few minutes later, the waiter _____ _____ the soup
                                        3.
to the table. The man _____ _____ ___, "Excuse me. Your
                            4.
finger is in my wife's soup." The waiter ___ ____ ____ __,
                                              5.
"Oh, that's OK. It isn't too hot."

2.

| ask | think | answer | say | be |

A woman _____ at the doctor's office.
                    1.
The doctor _____ her, "What's the trouble?"
                  2.
The woman _____, "I hurt everywhere. It hurts
                3.
when I touch my head. It hurts when I touch my leg, and it
hurts when I touch my arm." The doctor _____
                                              4.
for a moment. Then he _____, "I know what's
                          5.
wrong... Your finger is broken!"

3.

| tell | say | ask | look | see | stop |

A man _____ his car at a traffic light.
1.
A policeman stops next to him and _____ a
2.
penguin in the car. The policeman _____ the
3.
man, "You can't drive with a penguin in your car. Take that
penguin to the zoo." The man _____, "Yes, sir,
4.
I will." The next day, the policeman sees the man's car
again. And the penguin is still in the car. The policeman
_____, "Why do you have that penguin? I told you
5.
to take it to the zoo!" The man _____ at the policeman
6.
and says, "I did that, and we had a great time. Today we're going to
the movies."

Tip **Critical Thinking**

In Activity B, you
have to learn a joke
and tell it. **Restating**,
or saying something
again in your own
words, is a good way
to share information.

B. Work in a group. Choose a joke from Activity A. Study the joke and try to remember it. You can write some notes below to help you. Take turns telling the jokes using the simple present. Look at your classmates; don't read from your book.

_____

_____

_____

The **simple present third-person singular** form of a regular verb ends in either -s or -es.

> He eats a lot. She washes her hands.

The pronunciation of this final sound depends on the sound at the end of the base verb. There are three possible sounds:

- The -*s* = /z/ when the sound is **voiced** (with sound). This includes all vowel sounds, and the consonants: /b/, /d/, /g/, /l/, /m/, /n/, /ŋ/ (si**ng**), /r/, /ð/ (brea**th**, fa**th**er), and /v/.
- The -*s* = /s/ when the sound is **unvoiced** (without sound), including /f/, /k/, /p/, and /t/.
- The -*s*/-*es* = /əz/ when the final sound has an -*s* or -*z* like sound, including: /ʤ/ (ju**dg**e), /s/, /ʃ/ (wi**sh**), /tʃ/ (wat**ch**), and /z/.

CD 2
Track 24

Read and listen to the examples in the chart.

If the base verb ends in...	Base verb	*he/she/it*
a voiced sound, pronounce the third person singular with /z/	say	says
	tell	tells
	give	gives
	answer	answers
an unvoiced sound, pronounce the third person singular with /s/	laugh	laughs
	look	looks
	stop	stops
	eat	eats
an -s or -z like sound, pronounce the third person singular with /əz/	change	changes
	miss	misses
	wash	washes
	watch	watches

A. Read each joke and underline every third-person singular simple present verb. Write /z/, /s/, or /əz/ above each *-s* or *-es* to indicate the pronunciation.

1. **In the shop**

   A man walks into a shop and sees a little rabbit. He asks

   the shopkeeper, "Does your rabbit bite?"

   The shopkeeper says, "No, my rabbit doesn't bite."

   The man pets the rabbit, and the rabbit bites him.

   "Ouch!" He says, "You said your rabbit doesn't bite!"

   The shopkeeper replies, "That isn't my rabbit!"

 **for Success**

You can use the simple present third-person *-s* and *-es* pronunciation rules for the pronunciation of plural forms, too. For example, the plural of boot is boots. The *-s* is an unvoiced /s/ sound.

2. **At school**

   A five-year-old boy asks his teacher to help him put on his boots. The

   teacher says, "Of course," and she starts to help the boy. She pushes

   and pulls on the boots, but they don't go on the boy's feet. She gets very

   tired, so she takes a rest.

   The little boy says, "Teacher, these aren't my boots."

   "Why didn't you tell me?" the teacher asks.

   The boy replies, "They're my brother's boots. My mom made me wear

   them today."

   The teacher pushes and pulls on the boots some more, and finally, she

   gets them on the boy's feet.

   "OK! Now, where are your gloves?" she asks the boy.

   The boy answers, "I put them in my boots!"

B. Work with a partner. Take turns reading the jokes aloud. Use the correct pronunciation of the third-person singular endings.

When you tell a story or a joke, there are different ways to make it more interesting.

- **Make eye contact with the listener(s).** This will help you connect with your audience and keep them interested.
- **Use your voice to express different feelings.** This helps the listener understand the feelings of the people in the story.
- **Pause—stop speaking for a moment**—before you say the punch line (the end of a story or joke). This can help to make the ending a surprise.

CD 2
Track 25

Listen to the example.

...The man touches the rabbit, and the rabbit bites him.
"Ouch!" He says, "You said your rabbit doesn't bite!"

surprised/angry tone of voice

The shopkeeper replies, "That isn't my rabbit!"
↑
pause

CD 2
Track 26

A. Listen to the excerpts from the jokes. Underline the places where the speaker uses tone of voice. Draw an arrow (↑) where the speaker pauses.

1. One day, I'm at home. I turn on the TV and sit down on the sofa. My wife asks, "What are you doing?" I say, "Nothing." She says, "You did that yesterday." So I answer, "Yeah, I know. I wasn't finished."

2. A woman's at the doctor's office. The doctor asks her, "What's the trouble?" The woman answers, "I hurt everywhere. It hurts when I touch my head. It hurts when I touch my leg, and it hurts when I touch my arm." The doctor thinks for a moment. Then he says, "I know what's wrong... Your finger is broken!"

B. Work with a partner. Read the excerpts from Activity A aloud. Practice making eye contact, using tone of voice, and pausing.

C. Read these excerpts from jokes. Underline the places where you can use tone of voice. Draw an arrow (↑) where you can pause.

1. A few minutes later, the waiter brings the soup to the table. The man says, "Excuse me. Your finger is in my soup." The waiter replies, "Oh, that's OK. It isn't too hot."

2. The next day, the policeman sees the man's car again. The penguin is in the car. The policeman asks, "Why do you have that penguin? I told you to take it to the zoo." The man looks at the policeman and says, "Yes, thank you. I did that, and we had a great time! Today we're going to the movies!"

D. Work in a group. Take turns reading aloud the excerpts in Activity C. Remember to make eye contact, use tone of voice, and pause before the end.

| Unit Assignment | Tell a joke or a funny story |

 In this assignment, you are going to tell a funny story or joke to a group (or to the class). Use some of the tips from this unit to add interest and humor. Think about the question, "Who makes you laugh?" and refer to the Self-Assessment checklist on page 120 as you prepare to tell your joke or story.

For alternative unit assignments, see the *Q: Skills for Success Teacher's Handbook*.

CONSIDER THE IDEAS

Complete the tasks.

1. Read the joke and try to guess the punch line (the last line). Then listen to check your answer.

   A tourist visits Sydney, Australia. He wants to go to the beach. But he doesn't know how to get there. He sees a policeman. He waves to the policeman and says, "Excuse me! Can you help me?"

   The policeman comes over and says, "Yes, sir. How can I help you?"

   The tourist says, "Can you tell me the fastest way to get to the beach?"

The policeman asks, "Are you walking or driving?"

The tourist answers, "Driving."

The policeman answers, _____

_____ .

CD 2
Track 27

2. Listen to an Australian comedian tell the joke in task 1. Write the punch line.

CD 2
Track 28

3. Listen again and discuss these questions with a partner.
   a. Do you understand the joke?
   b. Do you think the comedian was good? Why or why not?
   c. Where in the joke did the comedian use tone of voice or pause? Underline where his tone of voice changed and draw an arrow (↑) where there was a pause.

PREPARE AND SPEAK

A. **GATHER IDEAS** Think of a joke or a funny story you want to tell. It can be a joke or a story you know or a funny story about something that happened to you or someone you know.

B. **ORGANIZE IDEAS** Make notes about your joke or story in your notebook. Remember that you can use the simple present. Then complete the tasks below.

1. Underline places in your joke or story where you can use tone of voice. Draw an arrow (↑) in places where you can pause.

2. Practice telling your jokes or stories with your partner. Use eye contact, tone of voice, and pauses to make the joke more interesting.

C. **SPEAK** Tell your joke or story to a group or to the class. Refer to the Self-Assessment checklist on page 120 before you begin.

CHECK AND REFLECT

A. **CHECK** Think about the Unit Assignment as you complete the Self-Assessment checklist.

SELF-ASSESSMENT		
Yes	**No**	
☐	☐	I was able to speak easily about the topic.
☐	☐	My partner/group/class understood me and thought I was funny.
☐	☐	I used simple present to tell a story/joke.
☐	☐	I used vocabulary from the unit.
☐	☐	I used eye contact, pause, and tone of voice when telling a story/joke.
☐	☐	I pronounced the third-person -s/-es correctly.

B. **REFLECT** Discuss these questions with a partner.

What is something new you learned in this unit?

 Think about the Unit Question, "Who makes you laugh?" Are there more people now who make you laugh? Who are they? Why do they make you laugh?

Track Your Success

Circle the words you learned in this unit.

Nouns
comedian
feelings 🔑
film 🔑
hit 🔑

Verb
imagine 🔑
understand 🔑

Adjectives
afraid 🔑
huge 🔑
powerful 🔑
professional 🔑
wrong 🔑

Adverbs
however 🔑
probably 🔑

Phrases
make eye contact
make fun of
sense of humor

🔑 Oxford 2000 keywords
AWL Academic Word List

Check (✓) the skills you learned. If you need more work on a skill, refer to the page(s) in parentheses.

LISTENING ⚪	I can listen for specific information. (p. 107)
VOCABULARY ⚪	I can recognize and use synonyms. (p. 111)
GRAMMAR ⚪	I can recognize and use the simple present for informal narratives. (p. 113)
PRONUNCIATION ⚪	I can recognize and use the simple present third person -s/-es. (p. 115)
SPEAKING ⚪	I can use eye contact, pause, and tone of voice. (p. 117)
LEARNING OUTCOME ⚪	I can use appropriate eye contact, tone of voice, and pauses to tell a funny story or a joke to my classmates.

LISTENING	●	listening for signal words
VOCABULARY	●	using the dictionary
GRAMMAR	●	gerunds as subjects or objects
PRONUNCIATION	●	questions of choice
SPEAKING	●	asking for and giving opinions

LEARNING OUTCOME

Participate in a group interview about how important music is in your lives.

Unit QUESTION

Why is music important to you?

PREVIEW THE UNIT

A Discuss these questions with your classmates.

How often do you listen to music?

What kind of music do you usually listen to?

Look at the photo. What are the women doing?

B Discuss the Unit Question above with your classmates.

Listen to *The Q Classroom*, Track 29 on CD 2, to hear other answers.

CD 2
Track 30

C **Do you know these types of music? Listen to the excerpts and number the type of music in the order you hear it.**

___ Classical   ___ Jazz

___ Pop   ___ Rock

D **Ask questions. Find a different classmate for each activity. Ask one follow-up question to get more information.**

A: Excuse me. Do you play a musical instrument?
B: Yes, I do.
A: Great. What do you play?

Find a classmate who...	Name	More information
1. plays a musical instrument		
2. listens to music while studying		
3. enjoys dancing		
4. likes the same music as you		
5. likes to sing		
6. listens to music while exercising		

E **What did you learn about your classmates? Share two things with the class.**

LISTENING 1 | Mind, Body, and Music

VOCABULARY

Tip for Success

Remember to use the context of the sentence to help you figure out the meaning of a new vocabulary word.

Here are some words from Listening 1. Read the sentences. Then write each bold word next to the correct definition.

1. Your **brain** holds information and feelings.

2. Paolo is a great musician. He can play five different **instruments**.

3. One **benefit** of listening to music is that it can make you feel happy and calm.

4. Steve is very **active**. He plays in two bands, and he belongs to a folk dance group, too.

5. Please turn off that loud music. I can't **concentrate** on my homework!

6. Listening to a lot of English songs can **improve** your English vocabulary.

7. Most **humans** live in cities.

8. Playing the drums is very good for you. When you hit the drum, it **lowers stress** and helps you feel good.

a. _____ (*phrase*) makes you feel more relaxed

b. _____ (*verb*) give all your attention to something

c. _____ (*noun*) something that is good or helpful

d. _____ (*noun*) the part inside a person's head that thinks and feels

e. _____ (*noun*) things that you use to play music

f. _____ (*adjective*) always busy, doing many things

g. _____ (*verb*) make something better

h. _____ (*noun*) people

PREVIEW LISTENING 1

Mind, Body, and Music

You are going to listen to a scientist giving a university lecture about the effects of music on the brain and why music is good for people.

Check (✓) the ways you think music helps people.

- ☐ work
- ☐ learning
- ☐ memory
- ☐ stress
- ☐ friendship
- ☐ physical problems

LISTEN FOR MAIN IDEAS

 CD 2
Track 31

Read the statements. Then listen to the lecture and check (✓) the benefits the speaker talks about.

____ a. Music makes people work harder.

____ b. Listening to music is helpful for learning.

____ c. Music can improve memory.

____ d. Playing music is a good way to make friends.

____ e. Music can help people who have physical problems.

____ f. Music can lower stress.

LISTEN FOR DETAILS

 CD 2
Track 32

Read the questions. Then listen again and circle the best answer to each.

1. What type of music is especially good for studying?
   a. rock
   b. classical
   c. jazz

2. What did the study show about children who learn to play music?
   a. Their brains are huge.
   b. They use their brains more.
   c. They do better in school.

3. How can doctors use music?
   a. They can help patients with brain diseases.
   b. They can study deep inside the brain.
   c. They can use it to remember patients' names.

4. How can music help older people?
   a. It helps them stay active.
   b. It helps prevent accidents.
   c. It helps them talk about their problems.

5. How does music help lower stress?
   a. It helps active people move more slowly.
   b. It helps people sleep longer.
   c. It slows down the heart and releases chemicals that relax us.

 WHAT DO YOU THINK?

Discuss the questions in a group.

1. Do you listen to music when you study? Do you think classical music is best?

2. Do you or someone you know use music to activate memories, stay active, or lower stress? Give an example.

3. What is one new thing you learned from this lecture?

| Listening Skill | Signal words and phrases | |

In a lecture, speakers use special words and phrases to **signal** when they introduce a new topic. If you learn these phrases, they will help you to follow a lecture or presentation better.

You will hear different phrases in different parts of the lecture.

At the beginning:	**First/First of all**, I'll talk about music and health.
	The first important benefit of music **is that** it can help us relax.
In the middle:	**The next thing I'll** talk about is the history of music.
	In addition, music helps people stay active.
	Also, listening to music can give us more energy.
At the end:	**The last/final topic is** how music helps us learn.
	Finally/Lastly, listening to music can make us feel happy.

A. Listen to the summary of a lecture about the benefits of music. Complete the summary with the words and phrases that you hear.

Tip for Success

When you take notes, it's helpful to listen for phrases such as *First...*, *The second..., One more..., In addition,* etc. These phrases can help you organize the speaker's main points.

1. _____ of music is that it can help us learn. Listening to music makes the brain active, so we can concentrate and learn better.

2. _____, music improves memory. Research shows that music can help people remember events and details from the past.

3. _____ music can help people with physical problems and can help older people stay active. It can also help people start to move again, even after many years of not moving.

4. _____, music can help to lower stress. Some types of music, such as classical music, cause the heart rate to slow down. And they cause the brain to release chemicals that relax us.

B. Work with a partner. Take turns reading your completed sentences from Activity A. Discuss any differences in your answers.

LISTENING 2 | Music in Our Lives

VOCABULARY

Here are some words from Listening 2. Read the definitions. Then complete each sentence with the correct word.

> **escape** (*verb*) to get free from someone or something
>
> **express** (*verb*) to say or show what you think or how you feel
>
> **forget** (*verb*) to stop thinking about something, to not remember
>
> **private** (*adjective*) for one person or a small group of people only
>
> **rhythm** (*noun*) a regular pattern of sounds that come again and again
>
> **team** (*noun*) a group of people who play a sport or game together
>
> **traditional** (*adjective*) old, from a long time ago
>
> **tune** (*noun*) a song

1. When I have a lot of stress and I need to _____, I go into my room and turn on my favorite music.

2. I love dancing to pop music. It has a great _____.

3. We can't go to the band's concert. It's _____. You need a special invitation.

4. Listening to music, singing, or dancing is a great way to _____ about stress.

5. Before we play a game, my baseball _____ sings our club song.

6. "Let It Be" is my favorite _____ by the Beatles.

7. My grandmother often sings _____ songs in Italian.

8. When I sing, I feel like I can _____ my true emotions.

PREVIEW LISTENING 2

Music in Our Lives

You are going to listen to four people talk about the importance of music in their lives. Read the statements. Which person said each? Match each statement to a photo.

a. Listening to my favorite song gives me energy.
b. Music brings my friends together. We're like a big family.
c. I think music is a really important part of my culture.
d. My music gives me a way to escape from the rest of the world.

Maria ____   Jamal ____   Yoshiko ____   Alex ____

LISTEN FOR MAIN IDEAS

CD 2 Track 34

Read the statements. Then listen to Maria, Jamal, Yoshiko, and Alex. Check (✓) the two reasons music is important to each of them.

1. Maria
   - ☐ a. It brings her friends together.
   - ☐ b. It helps her stay healthy.
   - ☐ c. It helps her express who she is.

2. Jamal
   - ☐ a. It helps him study.
   - ☐ b. It lowers stress.
   - ☐ c. It helps him forget about his problems.

3. Yoshiko
   - ☐ a. It's her favorite way to relax.
   - ☐ b. It helps her remember things.
   - ☐ c. It's an important part of her culture.

4. Alex
   - ☐ a. It gives him energy.
   - ☐ b. It helps him get ready to play soccer.
   - ☐ c. It makes him feel less stressed.

LISTEN FOR DETAILS

CD 2 Track 35

Read the questions. Then listen again and write answers. Write complete sentences.

1. What type of music does Maria usually listen to?

   _____

2. Where does she practice dancing with her friends?

   _____

3. What type of music does Jamal like to play and write?

   _____

4. Who does he say is his best friend?

   _____

5. What type of songs does Yoshiko like singing?

_____

6. Who does she say listens to traditional Japanese music?

_____

7. Where is Alex's favorite singer from?

_____

8. How does he feel after he hears his favorite song?

_____

 ## WHAT DO YOU THINK?

A. Discuss the questions in a group.

1. Do you share the people's feelings about music?

2. Which person are you most similar to? Why?

3. In what ways is music important in your life?

B. Think about Listening 1 and Listening 2 as you discuss the questions.

1. Look at the different types of music on page 124. Which types of music do you think are best for lowering stress? Which are best for studying? For exercising?

2. Do some songs or types of music bring you memories of events or people from the past? Explain.

The dictionary gives more than one **definition** for many words. Be sure to choose the definition that best fits the context in which you found the word.

For example, the word *benefit* has two meanings in the dictionary.

> **ben·e·fit¹** 🔑 AWL /ˈbɛnəfɪt/ *noun*
> **1** [*count*] something that is good or helpful:
> *What are the **benefits of** having a computer?* • *I did it **for your benefit*** (= to help you).
> **2** [*count, noncount*] (**POLITICS**, **BUSINESS**) money or other advantages that you get from your job, the government, or a company you belong to:
> *unemployment benefits* • *All our employees receive medical benefits in addition to their salary.*

You want the definition as used in this sentence:

> The first important **benefit** of music is that it can help us learn.

You can see that definition 1 is correct for this use of the word *benefit*.

All dictionary entries are from the *Oxford Basic American Dictionary for learners of English* © Oxford University Press 2011.

Tip **Critical Thinking**

In Activity A, you have to **determine** which definition is the best. You use the context to choose between the different meanings. Using context to determine meaning is one way to improve your vocabulary skills.

A. Read the sentences and the dictionary definitions. Write the number of the correct definition of each underlined word.

____ 1. For example, listening to <u>classical</u> music when we study activates both the left and the right sides of the brain.

> **clas·si·cal** AWL /ˈklæsɪkl/ *adjective*
> **1** in a style that people have used for a long time because they think it is good: *classical dance* ⊃ **SYNONYM traditional** ⊃ **ANTONYM modern**
> **2** (**MUSIC**) Classical music is written for instruments that are not electronic, and is considered to be serious and important: *I prefer rock to classical music.*
> **3** connected with ancient Greece or Rome: *classical Greek architecture*

____ 2. It's <u>special</u> because people don't play that kind of music anywhere else.

> **spe·cial¹** 🔑 /ˈspɛʃl/ *adjective*
> **1** not usual or ordinary; important for a reason: *It's my birthday today, so we're having a special dinner.*
> **2** for a particular person or thing: *He goes to a special school for deaf children.*

_____ **3.** My mother has an old Elvis Presley <u>record</u> from 1955.

re·cord[1] 🔑 /ˈrɛkərd/ *noun* [count]
1 notes about things that have happened: *Keep a record of all the money you spend.*
2 (**SPORTS**) the best, fastest, highest, lowest, etc. that has been done in a sport: *She holds the world record for long jump.* • *He did it in record time* (= very fast). • *She's hoping to break the record for the mile* (= to do it faster than anyone has done before).
3 (**MUSIC**) a thin, round piece of black plastic that makes music when you play it on a special machine (called a RECORD PLAYER): *He still has his old record collection.*

_____ **4.** Scientists have found very, very old <u>instruments</u> such as drums and flutes made of animal skins and bones.

in·stru·ment 🔑 /ˈɪnstrəmənt/ *noun* [count]
1 (**MUSIC**) a thing that you use for playing music: *Violins and trumpets are musical instruments.* • *What instrument do you play?*
2 a thing that you use for doing a special job: *surgical instruments* (= used by doctors)

_____ **5.** Tom is planning to <u>move</u> from Boston to Miami next year.

move[1] 🔑 /muv/ *verb* (**moves, mov·ing, moved**)
1 to go from one place to another; to change the way you are standing or sitting: *Don't get off the bus while it's moving.* • *We moved to the front of the theater.*
2 to put something in another place or another way: *Can you move your car, please?*
3 to go to live in another place: *They sold their house in Detroit and moved to Ann Arbor.*
4 to cause someone to have strong feelings, especially of sadness: *The news report moved me to tears.*

B. Compare your answers with a partner.

SPEAKING

Grammar — Gerunds as subjects or objects

A **gerund** is an *-ing* form of a verb that can take the place of a noun or pronoun. Because gerunds end in *-ing*, they may <u>look</u> like verbs, but they are not verbs. A gerund acts as a noun.

- Gerunds are often the **subject** of a sentence. Several verbs that express actions or states are commonly gerunds.

  Dancing is great exercise.
  Singing karaoke is a lot of fun.

- Gerunds can also be the **object** (a noun or noun phrase that follows a verb). Many common verbs allow gerunds, such as: *avoid, discuss, dislike, enjoy, hate, like, love,* and *prefer.*

  I **like singing** and **dancing** with my friends.
  My sister **enjoys listening** to music while she studies.
  I **hate singing** in front of people.
  Do you **prefer writing** songs or **singing** them?

CD 2 Track 36

A. Read the excerpts from Listening 2. Guess the missing gerunds. Then listen and complete the excerpts with the correct gerunds.

1. My friends and I have a dance group, and we get together and practice in the park sometimes. _____ to music brings my friends together. We're like a big family. When we hear a great new song, we share it with the rest of the group. Then we work on some dance moves together. _____ helps me express who I am.

2. I just enjoy _____ by myself. _____ songs and _____ my music lowers my stress. My music gives me a way to escape from the rest of the world. When I'm making music, I can forget about my problems and my worries.

3. _____ is really popular in Japan. I like _____

time with my friends at a "karaoke box." That's a place where you can

get a private room and sing together. It's my favorite way to relax. I prefer

_____ Japanese pop songs, but they have all kinds of music.

4. Before every game, I enjoy ____ _____ a few minutes to

myself—away from the rest of the team. I put on my headphones, and I

listen to the same song by my favorite singer, Pitty. She's a rock musician

from Brazil. _____ her music really energizes me.

B. Write five sentences about how music is important in your life. Use a gerund as a subject or object. Use a different verb for each sentence.

| hear | listen | sing | dance | play |

1. _____

2. _____

3. _____

4. _____

5. _____

C. Read your sentences aloud to a partner.

Intonation in questions of choice web+

Questions of choice ask a person to choose between two things. Questions of choice have rising-falling intonation at the end.

CD 2
Track 37

Listen and repeat these sentences.

Which do you like better, rock or pop?

Do you usually listen to new music or old music?

Do you prefer singing or dancing?

A. Read these questions. Check (✓) the ones that are questions of choice. Then listen and repeat each question. Notice the difference in intonation.

____ 1. Do you usually listen to music alone or with other people?

____ 2. What's your favorite type of music?

____ 3. What is an example of traditional music from your country?

____ 4. Is your favorite singer from your country or another country?

____ 5. When you study, do you listen to music, or do you prefer quiet?

____ 6. Do you enjoy singing in front of other people?

____ 7. Which kind of music do you like better, classical or pop?

____ 8. Do you prefer listening to music in English or in your own language?

B. Work with a partner. Take turns asking and answering the questions from Activity A. Remember to use rising-falling intonation for the questions of choice.

| Speaking Skill | Asking for and giving opinions | |

At school, work, and in our daily lives, we often ask for and give opinions. Knowing common phrases can help you understand more easily and speak more naturally.

Asking for opinions

Use these phrases when you want to know someone's opinion.

What do you think of Miley Cyrus's new CD?

How do you feel about Korean pop music?

Do you think she's a good singer?

Tom is an amazing dancer. **Don't you agree?**

Giving your opinion

Use these phrases when you want to give your opinion.

I think the Rolling Stones are the best rock band of all time.

I don't think this song is very good.

I feel that more young people should listen to traditional music.

In my opinion, the Black Eyed Peas are the best band.

A. Read the topics in the box. Choose three topics and write a question for each. Use the phrases in the Speaking Skill box on page 136.

Mozart	traditional music
opera music	folk dance
pop music	classical dance

1. _____ ?

2. _____ ?

3. _____ ?

B. Work with a partner. Take turns asking and answering each question in Activity A.

Unit Assignment | **Interview a group about musical preferences**

 In this assignment, you will brainstorm interview questions to ask your classmates. You will then answer questions about your own musical preferences and why music is important to you. As you prepare your interview, think about the Unit Question, "Why is music important to you?" and refer to the Self-Assessment checklist on page 138.

For alternative unit assignments, see the *Q: Skills for Success Teacher's Handbook*.

CONSIDER THE IDEAS

 CD 2 Track 39

Read the questions below. Listen to an interview with a university student about Turkish classical music. Check (✓) the questions you hear.

____ a. What do you think of pop music?

____ b. What kind of music do you like to listen to?

____ c. Why do you like it?

____ d. Do you like to sing?

____ e. Where do you like to listen to music?

____ f. Who are your favorite musicians?

PREPARE AND SPEAK

A. **GATHER IDEAS** Work in a group. Read the topics below. Brainstorm a list of questions you can ask to find out about your classmates' musical preferences.

- opinions about music
- ways music is important in their lives
- artists, groups, or songs they like or dislike
- music from different cultures
- traditional music
- music in English

B. **ORGANIZE YOUR IDEAS** As a group, choose five questions from your list to ask your classmates. In your notebook, make a chart like the one on page 124. Make just two columns. Write only the questions in the chart now. You will complete the Answers column when you interview your classmates.

C. **SPEAK** Follow these steps. Refer to the Self-Assessment checklist below before you begin your group interview.

1. Join your group with another group. Group A takes turns asking Group B questions. Write each member's answers in the chart. Then Group B interviews Group A.

2. Look at the answers in your chart. What groups or types of music are the most popular? Least popular? How is music important in your classmates' lives? Tell the class.

CHECK AND REFLECT

A. **CHECK** Think about the Unit Assignment as you complete the Self-Assessment checklist.

SELF-ASSESSMENT		
Yes	No	
☐	☐	I was able to speak easily about the topic.
☐	☐	My partner/group/class understood me.
☐	☐	I used gerunds as subjects and objects.
☐	☐	I used vocabulary from the unit.
☐	☐	I asked for and gave opinions.
☐	☐	I used correct intonation in questions of choice.

B. **REFLECT** Discuss these questions with a partner.

What is something new you learned in this unit?

 Think about the Unit Question, "Why is music important to you?" Is your answer different now than when you started this unit? If yes, how is it different? Why?

Track Your Success

Circle the words you learned in this unit.

Nouns
benefit AWL 🔑
brain 🔑
human 🔑
instrument 🔑
rhythm
team 🔑
tune 🔑

Verbs
concentrate AWL 🔑
escape 🔑
express
forget 🔑
improve 🔑

Adjectives
active 🔑
private 🔑
traditional AWL

Phrases
lower stress
Do you think...?
Don't you agree?
How do you feel
   about...?
I think...
I don't think...
I feel that...
In my opinion,...
What do you think
   of...?

🔑 Oxford 2000 keywords
AWL Academic Word List

Check (✓) the skills you learned. If you need more work on a skill, refer to the page(s) in parentheses.

LISTENING ○	I can listen for signal words. (p. 127)
VOCABULARY ○	I can choose the correct dictionary definition. (p. 132)
GRAMMAR ○	I can use and recognize gerunds as subjects or objects. (p. 134)
PRONUNCIATION ○	I can use correct intonation in questions of choice. (p. 135)
SPEAKING ○	I can ask for and give opinions. (p. 136)
LEARNING OUTCOME ○	I can participate in a group interview about how important music is in our lives.

UNIT **8**

Honesty

LISTENING	●	making inferences
VOCABULARY	●	percentages and fractions
GRAMMAR	●	conjunctions *and* and *but*
PRONUNCIATION	●	linking consonants to vowels
SPEAKING	●	sourcing information

Conduct a survey to gather opinions on honesty and dishonesty, and then report your results to the class.

Unit QUESTION

When is honesty important?

PREVIEW THE UNIT

Ⓐ Discuss these questions with your classmates.

What are some examples of honest things that people do?

What are some examples of dishonest things that people do?

Look at the photo. What is the student doing?

Ⓑ Discuss the Unit Question above with your classmates.

⏵) Listen to *The Q Classroom*, Track 2 on CD 3, to hear other answers.

141

C Look at the survey below. How wrong are these actions? Check (✓) your opinion.

Are you honest?

Answer the eight questions to
see how honest you are!

	Not Wrong	A little wrong	Very wrong
1. Saying you are younger or older than you really are	○	○	○
2. Borrowing something from a friend or family member without asking	○	○	○
3. Sharing quiz or test answers with a classmate	○	○	○
4. Parking in a no-parking zone	○	○	○
5. Finding money on the street and keeping it	○	○	○
6. Copying a school report from the Internet	○	○	○
7. Getting music or movies from the Internet without paying	○	○	○
8. Going in front of a long line of people without waiting	○	○	○

Results

Tip Critical Thinking

In Activity C, you
have to **judge** an
action. **Judging**
right or wrong is an
important critical
thinking skill and it
helps you share your
opinions in Activity D.

D Work with a partner. Share your opinions about the actions in Activity C.

A: I think <u>saying you are younger or older than you really are</u> is very wrong.

B: I think it's only a little wrong.

LISTENING 1 | Dishonesty in Schools

VOCABULARY

Here are some words from Listening 1. Read the sentences. Write each bold word next to the correct definition.

1. He didn't study but he got an *A* on the test. Did he **cheat**?

2. The teacher took a **survey** to find out how many students use the Internet. All of the students answered *yes*.

3. **According to** a magazine article, most people tell lies sometimes.

4. Recent **technology**, such as the Internet and cell phones, makes communication fast and easy.

5. About **a quarter** of the class is international students.

6. Many musicians want to **prevent** people from getting music for free on the Internet.

7. I want to get a good **grade** on my final exam in math.

8. I feel sad when I hear stories about children who don't have enough food. I think it's wrong for children to **suffer**.

a. _____ (*noun*) the number or letter that shows how well you have done in school

b. _____ (*verb*) to do something that is not honest or fair

c. _____ (*noun*) questions to find out what people think or do

d. _____ (*noun*) knowledge about science and about how things work

e. _____ (*noun*) twenty-five percent

f. _____ (*verb*) to feel pain, sadness, or another unpleasant feeling

g. _____ (*phrase*) as something or someone says

h. _____ (*verb*) to stop someone from doing something or to stop something from happening

PREVIEW LISTENING 1

Dishonesty in Schools

You are going to listen to a TV news report about cheating in schools. What percentage of U.S. high school students do you think say they cheat?

☐ 25%   ☐ 50%   ☐ 75%

LISTEN FOR MAIN IDEAS

 CD 3
Track 3

Read the paragraphs. Then listen and check (✓) the paragraph that best summarizes the main idea of the news report.

____ 1. Many countries have problems with cheating. Some universities in China stop wireless phone messages, so students can't send text messages.

____ 2. Cheating is a problem in many schools. New technology makes it easier to cheat. Schools and teachers are thinking of ways to stop cheating.

____ 3. Teachers believe their students are honest, so they feel upset when students cheat. Students who cheat receive a zero on their work.

LISTEN FOR DETAILS

 CD 3
Track 4

Read the sentences. Then listen again and circle the best answer to complete each sentence.

1. According to the survey, 75 percent of (high school / university) students cheat in school.

2. The survey found that (less than / more than) half of students copy reports from the Internet.

3. The reporter is interviewing teachers at a (high school / university).

4. Some of Ms. Smith's students used cell phones to (send messages / call classmates) with the test answers.

5. Ms. Smith thinks it may be (possible / impossible) to prevent students from using the Internet or sending text messages.

6. A university in (China / Europe) put cameras in all of its classrooms.

 **WHAT DO YOU THINK?**

Discuss the questions in a group.

1. According to the teachers in the news story, why is cheating bad?

2. Do you think cheating is a problem in schools? Why or why not?

3. Do you think it is possible to stop students from cheating? How?

| Listening Skill | Making inferences | |

Sometimes speakers don't give their opinions directly. To understand what a speaker thinks or feels about a topic, we need to "read between the lines," or use the context to decide what the speaker is really saying. We call this **making an inference**. For example, in Listening 1 one of the teachers is speaking about her students' cheating.

> Well, I didn't want to believe it at first. They were students I thought were truthful.

She doesn't say directly how she felt about the cheating, but you can understand that she felt sad or upset.

You can also make inferences about people's attitudes by listening for tone of voice.

 CD 3
Track 5

A. Listen to the excerpts from Listening 1. Circle the correct statement.

1. Wendy Smith
   a. thinks technology is the cause of cheating.
   b. does not allow students to use the Internet.

2. Wendy Smith
   a. doesn't believe her high school students.
   b. believes students who cheat will suffer.

3. Don Quinn
   a. thinks it's OK to copy from the Internet.
   b. doesn't think his students cheat.

4. Don Quinn
   a. doesn't think cheating is a big problem at the school.
   b. wants to put cameras in the classrooms.

5. Wendy Smith
   a. disagrees with Don Quinn.
   b. thinks students shouldn't get grades.

B. Compare answers with a partner. Explain the reasons for your answers in Activity A. What information helped you get the answers? Listen again if necessary.

LISTENING 2 | What's the Right Thing to Do?

VOCABULARY

Here are some words from Listening 2. Read the sentences. Circle the best definition for each bold word.

1. If you find money in the street, I think you should take it to the police. Even if it's just **a little bit** of money.
   a. a large amount
   b. a small amount

2. I found a great article online. Is it OK to use part of it in my report? I don't want to use the whole article—just a **section** of it.
   a. a part of something
   b. all of something

3. I'll finish my final report this week. It's a 20-page paper, and I have 15 pages **so far**.
   a. until now
   b. last year

4. Police officers have a big **responsibility**. They have to keep the city and its people safe.
   a. a free-time activity
   b. an important job to do

5. To tell a **lie** is not an honest thing to do.
   a. something you say that you know is not true
   b. something you say to appreciate another person

6. It only costs around one dollar to **download** a song on this website.
   a. make a copy from the Internet
   b. put a picture on the Internet

7. Sorry. You can't park here. It's **illegal**. This is a no-parking zone.
   a. OK sometimes
   b. not allowed by law

8. Teachers don't really know how many of their students cheat. That's because many students cheat on tests, but they don't **get caught**.
   a. be found doing something wrong
   b. find a report on the Internet

PREVIEW LISTENING 2

What's the Right Thing to Do?

You are going to listen to three conversations. One conversation is about school, one is about getting a job, and one is about using the Internet. What are ways people are sometimes dishonest in those situations? Add one idea to each.

At school: _sharing test answers,_ _____

_____

Getting a job: _lying about your education,_ _____

_____

Using the Internet: _putting false information on a website,_ ____

_____

LISTEN FOR MAIN IDEAS

CD 3
Track 6

Read the items. Then listen to the conversations. Circle the answer that tells what each person did.

1. André
   a. copied his friend's test answers.
   b. copied his friend's report.
   c. copied articles from the Internet.

2. Stephen
   a. told a lie to his manager at work.
   b. gave false information on his resume.
   c. made a mistake when he was a server.

3. A woman
   a. downloaded 24 articles without paying.
   b. sold music on the Internet for two million dollars.
   c. downloaded 24 songs without paying.

LISTEN FOR DETAILS

CD 3
Track 7

Read the items. Then listen again and circle the answer that best completes each sentence.

1. André is writing a report about
   a. languages in different countries.
   b. education in England.
   c. English education in different countries.

2. For his report, André used
   a. sections of different articles.
   b. a whole article.
   c. two different articles.

3. At Horizon Restaurant, Stephen was a
   a. server.
   b. manager.
   c. server and manager.

4. Stephen thinks what he did
   a. is very wrong.
   b. isn't really a lie.
   c. probably won't help him get the job.

5. According to the article, the woman had to pay
   a. $80,000 for each song.
   b. $8,000 for each song.
   c. $80 million total.

6. At the end of the conversation, Drew thinks
   a. downloading music without paying for it is wrong.
   b. downloading music without paying for it isn't so wrong.
   c. musicians make too much money.

 **WHAT DO YOU THINK?**

A. Discuss the questions in a group.

1. What is your opinion about these actions? Do you think they are wrong?
   - copying a report from the Internet
   - giving false information on a resume
   - downloading music from the Internet

2. Is it always better to be honest? Explain.

B. Think about both Listening 1 and Listening 2 as you discuss the questions.

1. Why do you think people sometimes cheat or are dishonest?

2. Give your opinion about these statements:

   It's OK to tell a lie when the truth might hurt someone's feelings.

   You have to be a little dishonest to be a successful person.

| Vocabulary Skill | Percentages and fractions | |

Percentages and fractions are different ways of talking about an amount that is part of a whole (one half, 50 percent). When you give survey results or facts from an article, it's helpful to understand and know how to say numbers in these ways.

You can express amounts as either percentages or fractions. Here are some common examples:

(25%) twenty-five percent	=	(1/4) a quarter/one quarter
(33%) thirty-three percent	=	(1/3) a third/one third
(50%) fifty percent	=	(1/2) a half/one half
(66%) sixty-six percent	=	(2/3) two thirds
(75%) seventy-five percent	=	(3/4) three quarters

A. Listen and complete the excerpts from Listening 1 with the correct percentage or fraction. Use words, not numbers.

1. A recent survey in the U.S. found that about

   _____ of high school students cheat in school.

   They share test answers, look at classmates' test papers, and send text

   messages with answers during a test. And according to the survey, more

   than _____ of students also copy reports from

   the Internet.

2. Last year, about _____ of my students turned in

   final reports that they copied from the Internet.

3. I read an article about what schools in other countries are doing. The

   article said that in one African country, the government canceled about

   _____ of test scores after students cheated on tests.

4. And a university in Europe did a survey on cheating. According to the

   survey, _____ of students answered that they

   cheated. So the university put cameras in all of its classrooms.

B. Rewrite each amount from Activity A. Use numbers.

1. _____

2. _____

3. _____

4. _____

SPEAKING

Grammar   Conjunctions *and* and *but*

> You can use the conjunction *and* to join two ideas or add another.
>
> ⌈ Seventy-five percent of high school students say they cheat, **and** more
> ⌊ than half say they copy reports from the Internet.
>
> The conjunction *but* connects two opposite ideas.
>
> ⌈ Some people think it's OK to download music without paying for it from
> ⌊ the Internet, **but** it's illegal.

A. Complete the sentences with *and* or *but*. Then read your sentences to a partner.

1. Jane put false information on her resume. It says she has a college

    degree, _____ she really doesn't.

2. Brian's going to get in trouble someday. He downloads music from the

    Internet without paying, _____ he downloads movies, too.

3. Once I found a wallet on the bus. It didn't have any money in it,

    _____ it had a lot of credit cards. I took it to the police

    station, _____ they returned it to the owner.

4. It's OK to use sections of an Internet article in your paper,

    _____ you need to give the author's name,

    _____ you should also give the website where you found it.

5. I try to be honest all the time, _____ sometimes

    it's impossible.

6. Mr. Markus is a very good businessman. His products are excellent,

    _____ his prices are fair.

7. Students who cheat may do well on tests, _____ they may

    get good grades, _____ they don't learn anything.

8. You shouldn't lie about your experience to get a job. Your boss might

find out, _____ you'll lose your job.

B. Circle either *and* or *but* and then complete each sentence with your own idea.

1. Some people say it's OK to be a little dishonest in business, (and /(but))

   _I do not think that is right._____ _____ _____

2. He uses a younger photo of himself on his Web page, (and / but) _____

   _____

3. I found some money in the street, (and / but) _____

   _____

4. It's easy to download music from free websites, (and / but) _____

   _____

5. She gave her homework to a classmate, (and / but) _____

   _____

6. He lied about breaking the vase, (and / but) _____

   _____

C. Read your sentences to a partner.

Pronunciation	Linking consonants to vowels	web

Speakers often connect the sounds between words. This is called **linking**. One way they do this is by linking a word that ends in a consonant sound to a word after it that begins with a vowel sound.

CD 3
Track 9

Listen to these phrases.

because of	quiz answers	false information
a third of	not acceptable	have a lot of

A. Listen to the sentences. Show the linked consonant and vowel sounds by connecting the letters.

1. I think a lot of people lie about their age.

2. Is it OK to keep money that you find in the street?

3. About a quarter of the students in the class cheated on the test.

4. Do you think it's OK to call in sick to work if you're not sick?

5. Because of the Internet, musicians and bands don't make as much money.

6. In our English class, it's not OK to use an article from the Internet without giving credit.

B. Work with a partner. Take turns reading the sentences from Activity A. Practice linking the consonants and vowel sounds.

| Speaking Skill | Sourcing information | |

Sometimes you need to include information that you get from the Internet, a newspaper or magazine article, a radio news report, or a survey. It's important to give this information the right way in research reports or class discussions. You must name the source of your information. Here are some useful phrases to refer to a source of information.

According to the	survey, article, website,	75 percent of students cheat.
The survey The results	found that showed that	some people are honest. most people are honest.
More than half About 75 percent	answered said	yes / no. that they sometimes lie.

CD 3
Track 11

A. The results of the magazine survey are in! Match the survey results to the phrases on the left. (Make guesses.) Then listen and check your answers.

Tip for Success

To avoid plagiarism, always use quotation marks ("...") around anything that comes directly from a text. Be sure to give the source.

Survey Results!

People surveyed ...	do this!?
____1. More than half	a. give false information on a resume.
____2. Over ten percent	b. sometimes change the price tag to a lower price for something they want to buy.
____3. About 20%	c. take paper or pens from their company to use at home.
____4. About 60%	d. sometimes lie to friends or family to avoid hurting their feelings.
____5. Three quarters	e. call in sick to work when they aren't sick.

B. Work with a partner. Talk about the survey results in Activity A. Use the phrases from the Speaking Skill box on page 153.

The survey found that more than half of the people...

In this assignment, you are going to survey your classmates about their opinions on honesty and dishonesty. Then you will report your survey results to the class. As you prepare your survey, think about the Unit Question, "When is honesty important?" and refer to the Self-Assessment checklist on page 156.

For alternative unit assignments, see the *Q: Skills for Success Teacher's Handbook*.

CONSIDER THE IDEAS

CD 3
Track 12

Listen to Scott's honesty survey report of his classmates. Complete the missing percentages.

Scott Jones
Honesty Survey Report
English 101
Honesty Survey Results

1. How important do you think honesty is?

    ___ % very important

    _36_% a little important

    ____% not important

2. Are you honest all the time?

    ____% yes ____% no

3. How wrong do you think these actions are?

    · not returning a library book

      ____% not wrong _61_% a little wrong ____% very wrong

    · hitting a car in a parking lot and not telling the owner

      ____% not wrong _3_% a little wrong ____% very wrong

    · cheating on a test

      _9_% not wrong ____% a little wrong ____% very wrong

PREPARE AND SPEAK

A. **GATHER IDEAS** Complete the activities.

1. Write five survey questions to ask your classmates about honesty. Use *Yes/No* questions (as in number 2 of Scott's survey) and multiple choice questions (as in numbers 1 and 3).

2. Work with a partner to test your questions. Ask your partner the questions and make changes if necessary.

B. **ORGANIZE IDEAS** Ask your five survey questions to ten people. Record each person's answers. When you finish, count the number of answers for each question. Write your survey results as percentages.

C. **SPEAK** Work in a group. Report the results of your honesty survey. Refer to the Self-Assessment checklist below before you begin. Use the percentages and fractions, and use phrases that source the results of your survey.

CHECK AND REFLECT

A. **CHECK** Think about the Unit Assignment as you complete the Self-Assessment checklist.

SELF-ASSESSMENT		
Yes	No	
☐	☐	I was able to speak easily about the topic.
☐	☐	My partner/group/class understood me.
☐	☐	I used *and* and *but* correctly.
☐	☐	I used vocabulary from the unit.
☐	☐	I used phrases to source information.
☐	☐	I linked consonants to vowels.

B. **REFLECT** Discuss these questions with a partner.

What is something new you learned in this unit?

 Think about the Unit Question, "When is honesty important?" Is your answer different now than when you started this unit? If yes, how is it different? Why?

Track Your Success

Circle the words you learned in this unit.

Nouns
grade 🔑 AWL
lie 🔑
responsibility 🔑
section 🔑 AWL
survey AWL
technology 🔑 AWL

Verbs
cheat 🔑
download
prevent 🔑
suffer 🔑

Adjective
illegal 🔑 AWL

Percentages and Fractions
a quarter 🔑
twenty-five percent
fifty percent
seventy-five percent
thirty-three percent
sixty-six percent

Phrases
according to 🔑
a little bit
get caught
so far
About 75 percent said...
More than half answered...
The survey found that...
The survey showed that...

🔑 Oxford 2000 keywords
AWL Academic Word List

Check (✓) the skills you learned. If you need more work on a skill, refer to the page(s) in parentheses.

LISTENING	●	I can make inferences. (p. 145)
VOCABULARY	●	I can recognize and use percentages and fractions. (p. 149)
GRAMMAR	●	I can recognize and use the conjunctions *and* and *but*. (p. 151)
PRONUNCIATION	●	I can link consonants to vowels. (p. 152)
SPEAKING	●	I can refer to a source of information. (p. 153)
LEARNING OUTCOME	●	I can conduct a survey to gather opinions on honesty and dishonesty, and then report my results to the class.

UNIT **9**

Life Changes

LISTENING	● listening for different opinions
VOCABULARY	● verb + noun collocations
GRAMMAR	● imperative of *be* + adjective
PRONUNCIATION	● content word stress in sentences
SPEAKING	● checking for listeners' understanding

LEARNING OUTCOME

Deliver a presentation providing instructions on how a person can make a change in his/her life.

Unit QUESTION

Is it ever too late to change?

PREVIEW THE UNIT

A Discuss these questions with your classmates.

Do you like to make changes in your life, or do you prefer things to stay the same?

Do you think old people or young people find it easier to make changes in their lives? Why?

Look at the photo. Do you think the woman is finding it easy to change her life?

B Discuss the Unit Question above with your classmates.

Listen to *The Q Classroom*, Track 13 on CD 3, to hear other answers.

C Check (✓) the changes in your life. Then write when the change happened.

Change	When it happened
☐ moved to a new house or apartment	
☐ changed schools	
☐ started high school	
☐ started university	
☐ moved to a new city or town	
☐ started a new job or career	
☐ started a new hobby or sport	
☐ stopped a bad habit	
☐ moved to a different country	
☐ got married	
☐ had a child	

D Tell a partner about your changes. Were the changes easy or difficult for you?

I changed schools last year. It was a little difficult because...

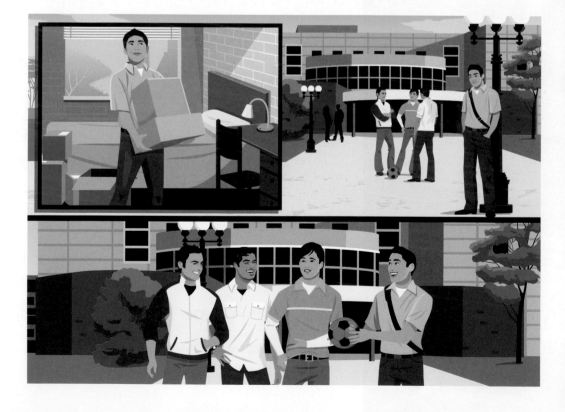

LISTENING

LISTENING 1 | Attitudes about Change

VOCABULARY

Here are some words and phrases from Listening 1. Read the definitions. Then complete each sentence with the correct word or phrase.

> **accept** (*verb*) to say yes to something
>
> **change your mind** (*verb*) to decide to do something differently, to change your plan
>
> **especially** (*adverb*) more than usual or more than others
>
> **flexible** (*adjective*) able to change easily
>
> **opportunity** (*noun*) a chance to do something
>
> **progress** (*noun*) improvement or development
>
> **proverb** (*noun*) a popular saying that many people know and say, which teaches an important lesson
>
> **remain** (*verb*) to stay in the same way, not to change

1. My boss dislikes any kind of change. It's difficult for her to

    _____ new ideas.

2. Life changes can be difficult, _____ big changes like

    moving to a new country.

3. My school has a study abroad program in London. I'm definitely going

    to go. It's a really good _____ to improve my English.

4. Karen did much better in school this year. She studied hard and made

    _____ in all her classes.

5. Greg hates any kind of change. He really needs to learn to be more

    _____.

6. I learned a Chinese _____ about change today. It says,

    "A journey of a thousand miles begins with one step."

7. Are you still planning to move to a new apartment this summer, or did you _____?

8. Everything changes. Nothing can _____ the same for very long.

PREVIEW LISTENING 1

Attitudes about Change

You are going to listen to a group of international university students discussing proverbs about change. What do you think these proverbs mean? Match each proverb to its meaning.

____ 1. Life is what you make of it.

____ 2. You can't teach an old dog new tricks.

____ 3. It's never too late to change.

____ 4. All change is progress.

a. You can change at any age if you want to.

b. You can do anything you want to in life.

c. You can't change easily after a certain age.

d. Change is always good.

LISTEN FOR MAIN IDEAS

CD 3
Track 14

Read the statements. Then listen and check (✓) the statement that is true about the students.

____ a. They agree with all of the proverbs.

____ b. They don't like to make changes in their lives.

____ c. They are happy they came to the U.S. to study.

____ d. They are afraid to move to another country.

LISTEN FOR DETAILS

 CD 3
Track 15 **Listen again. Complete each proverb. Then write the country each is from.**

1. An old _____ will not learn how to _____.

   Country: _____

2. One who _____ look ahead _____ behind.

   Country: _____

3. A _____ man changes his mind, but a fool _____.

   Country: _____

4. To change and to _____ are two _____ things.

   Country: _____

Q WHAT DO YOU THINK?

Discuss the questions in a group.

1. Which proverb from the listening do you like best? Why?

2. What do the students agree is important for people to do if they want to improve their lives?

3. What do people think about change in your culture? Is it a positive thing or a negative thing? Do you agree?

People express different **opinions** when they speak. Listening for the phrases or expressions that a speaker uses will help you to know when a speaker is agreeing or disagreeing. If you learn these expressions, you can participate more easily in discussions and add your own opinions.

Agreement

When speakers agree with an opinion or idea, they often use these expressions:

I totally agree.	You're right.
I think so, too.	That's true.
Me, too.	
Definitely!	

Disagreement

Speakers sometimes disagree directly. But it is more common to use indirect expressions because they sound more polite.

Direct		**Indirect (more polite)**
I disagree.	→	I'm not sure I agree.
I don't think so.	→	I don't know if I agree.
That's not true.	→	I don't know about that.

 CD 3
Track 16

A. Listen to the excerpts from Listening 1 and write the missing expressions.

Andrea: It means that when we get older, it's more difficult to change.

Older people don't want to change their thinking or their lifestyle.

They like things to stay the same.

Franco: _____. I think older people can change.
₁

Everyone can change. It's important to be flexible at any age.

Franco: In Brazil we say, "One who does not look ahead, remains behind." This means it's important to accept new ideas. You should always be ready to change.

Juan Carlos: _____. In Spain, we say, "A wise man
                                          2
changes his mind, but a fool never will."

Juan Carlos: It's always good to make a change. Like the proverb from the homework says, "All change is progress."

Katrina: Hmm. _____. Change isn't *always* good.
                                  3

Katrina: We should be careful when we change things. First, we should be sure the change will make things better.

Franco: _____. The important thing is that we *can*
                              4
change—I mean improve—if we want to.

B. Work with a partner. Discuss each statement. Agree or disagree using the expressions from the Listening Skill box on page 164. Give reasons for your opinion.

1. Older people can't change.

2. People can't change their personalities.

3. Big life changes are stressful.

4. The world isn't changing for the better.

5. Change isn't always good.

6. If something works well, you shouldn't change it—even if you can improve it.

LISTENING 2 | Tips from a Life Coach

VOCABULARY

Here are some words from Listening 2. Read the sentences. Circle the answer that best defines each bold word.

1. Some **habits** are hard to change. For example, biting your fingernails or eating sweets.
   a. actions you dislike
   b. actions you do often

2. Many people want to lose weight. They may start a diet, but they often fail because they can't **stick to** it.
   a. continue
   b. begin

3. If you want to change the world, start with yourself. I think that's good **advice**.
   a. something that you say to help someone decide what to do
   b. something that you do to help someone

4. Can you **recommend** a good computer program for learning Spanish?
   a. to teach someone about something
   b. to tell someone that a person or a thing is good or useful

5. I'm taking guitar lessons. My **goal** is to start a band someday.
   a. something that you don't like
   b. something that you want to do

6. I hope I don't forget our exercise class on Tuesday. Can you please call me to **remind** me about it?
   a. help someone find something
   b. help someone remember something

7. A good teacher should **encourage** the students and help them improve.
   a. help someone continue something
   b. help someone stop something

8. Don't give up! If you work hard, you can **achieve** anything you want to.
   a. do or finish
   b. forget

PREVIEW LISTENING 2

Tips from a Life Coach

You will listen to a radio call-in show with professional life coach Diana Carroll. What do you think a life coach does?

LISTEN FOR MAIN IDEAS

CD 3
Track 17

Listen and check (✓) the show summary that best describes the radio call-in show.

WOUP Radio
Show Summary
August 16–21

____ 1. On today's show, life coach Diana Carroll talks about how she started her career and gives advice to people who want to become a life coach.

____ 2. This week, life coach Diana Carroll gives several callers advice about how to stop bad habits like overeating and watching too much TV.

____ 3. Life coach Diana Carroll joins the show. She tells us what a life coach does and helps one caller set goals to start a healthy lifestyle.

LISTEN FOR DETAILS

CD 3
Track 18

Listen again. What advice does Diana give to people who want to make a change? Complete the missing information.

1. Set _____ goals for yourself.

2. _____ your goals.

3. Share your _____ with someone.

4. Set a _____ to complete your goal.

5. _____ your success!

 **WHAT DO YOU THINK?**

A. Discuss the questions in a group.

1. Did you ever try to change a habit? What was the habit? Were you successful?

2. Would you like to try using a life coach? Why or why not?

B. Think about Listening 1 and Listening 2 as you discuss the questions.

1. Is it easy for you to make big changes in your life, for example, changing your home, school, or job? How do you feel when you make these types of changes?

2. What are some things you'd like to change in your life? Make notes in your notebook. Then share your answers.

Collocations are words that you often find together. For example, certain verbs go together with certain nouns in collocations like *make changes* or *set a goal*. You can improve your vocabulary if you learn new collocations and use them when you speak.

Some verbs go together with different nouns.

 for Success

A collocations dictionary lists English collocations alphabetically for easy reference.

change	
change one's attitude	The car accident **changed her attitude** about life.
change one's mind	Did you **change your mind** about moving?
make	
make a change	I need to **make some changes** in my life.
make progress	Kelly is **making a lot of progress** in math.

Some nouns go together with several verbs.

advice	
follow advice	Abbas didn't **follow his friend's advice**.
give advice	Parents often **give advice** to their children.
goal	
achieve a goal	If you work hard, you can **achieve any goal**.
set a goal	It's important to **set small goals**.

CD 3
Track 19

A. Read the excerpts from Listening 1 and Listening 2. Complete the excerpts with the missing collocations. Then listen and check your answers.

1. Some people want to make really big changes in their lives, for example, to find a new job or career, or to move to a new city. Others want to break bad habits, such as overeating or watching too much TV. And other people want to change their _____ about life in general—for example, they want to become more friendly or more flexible.

2. You need to share your goal with someone—for example, a co-worker or a friend...someone who can help you _____ your goal.

3. I give _____ to people who want to make changes in their lives.

4. In Spain, we say, "A wise man changes his _____, but a fool never will."

5. Many people want to change their lives, but they aren't sure how to get started. Or maybe they are able to make a _____, but they can't stick to it.

6. And we made a lot of _____ in our English... That's definitely a change for the better!

7. Thank you so much. You really helped me today. I'm definitely going to follow your _____.

8. The first step is to set small _____ for yourself. Many people try to make too many big changes quickly.

B. Write five questions about change to ask a partner. Use one of the collocations from the chart in each question.

1. _____

2. _____

3. _____

4. _____

5. _____

C. Ask and answer your questions from Activity B with a partner.

SPEAKING

When you give advice to someone, you can use the **imperative** of *be* + **adjective**. The imperative is the same as the base form of the verb.

☐ **Be** ready. **Be** careful.

When you give negative advice, use ***don't be*** + **adjective**.

☐ **Don't be** afraid.

To give more detailed advice, you can add ***to*** + **infinitive** to many adjectives.

Be ready **to change** your goals.

imperative adjective infinitive

Be careful **to check** your progress. Don't be afraid **to ask** for advice.

A. Read the article about how to start a new career. Underline the examples of *be* + adjective.

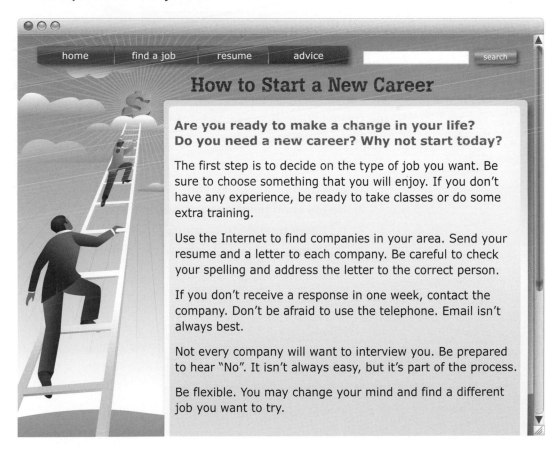

home | find a job | resume | advice | search

How to Start a New Career

Are you ready to make a change in your life? Do you need a new career? Why not start today?

The first step is to decide on the type of job you want. Be sure to choose something that you will enjoy. If you don't have any experience, be ready to take classes or do some extra training.

Use the Internet to find companies in your area. Send your resume and a letter to each company. Be careful to check your spelling and address the letter to the correct person.

If you don't receive a response in one week, contact the company. Don't be afraid to use the telephone. Email isn't always best.

Not every company will want to interview you. Be prepared to hear "No". It isn't always easy, but it's part of the process.

Be flexible. You may change your mind and find a different job you want to try.

B. Work with a partner. Imagine you are a life coach. Take turns giving the advice from Activity A. Look at the article if you need to, but be sure to make eye contact with your partner.

C. Write advice about how to be a better English student. Remember to use *be* (or *don't be*) + adjective + infinitive. Then share your advice with a partner. Use the adjectives in the box or your own ideas.

afraid	careful	prepared	ready	sure

1. _____

2. _____

3. _____

4. _____

5. _____

Pronunciation | **Content word stress in sentences**

Content words are the words that have the most meaning in a sentence. They are usually *nouns*, *main verbs*, *adverbs*, and *adjectives*. We usually stress the content words in a sentence. We say the stressed words a little more loudly and strongly than the other words in the sentence. In the proverbs below, the content words are bold.

CD 3
Track 20

Listen and pay attention to the word stress.

1. **Life** is what you **make** of it.
2. **Be** the **change** you **want** to **see** in the **world**.
3. It's **never** too **late** to **change**.
4. To **change** and to **improve** are two **different things**.

CD 3
Track 21

A. Circle the content words in these proverbs. Then listen and check the stress.

1. To learn is to change.

2. A change is as good as a rest.

3. Change your thoughts, and you change your world.

4. To improve is to change; to be perfect is to change often.

5. When the music changes, so does the dance.

6. You change your life by changing your heart.

CD 3
Track 22

B. Listen again and repeat the proverbs in Activity A. Then discuss the meaning of the proverbs with a partner.

Speaking Skill | **Checking for listeners' understanding**

When you give instructions or an explanation, it's helpful to stop and **check that the listener understands** everything. Here are some expressions you can use to check other people's understanding.

> Does everyone understand?
> Does that make sense?
> Is that clear?
> Are there any questions?

 for Success

It's polite to acknowledge an audience member's question before you answer it. Speakers often use expressions like: *That's an excellent question. / Thank you for asking that. / Good question.*

A. Look back at Activity C on page 172 and think about places where you can stop to check for listeners' understanding.

B. Work in a group. Take turns giving your instructions for how to be a better English student. Remember to stop and check for listeners' understanding.

In this assignment, you will choose a topic and give your classmates instructions on how to make a specific change in their lives. As you prepare to speak, think about the Unit Question, "Is it ever too late to change?" and refer to the Self-Assessment checklist on page 176.

For alternative unit assignments, see the *Q: Skills for Success Teacher's Handbook.*

CONSIDER THE IDEAS

 CD 3
Track 23

Listen to Mei Ling's instructions for how to break the habit of watching too much TV. Number the steps in the correct order.

How to Break the Habit of Watching Too Much TV

____ Add one more activity into your schedule every week.

____ Write a list of other activities you like to do.

____ Choose one or two hours when you usually watch TV. Write down a different activity.

____ Set a goal to watch less TV.

____ Celebrate when you achieve your goal.

____ Make a TV schedule.

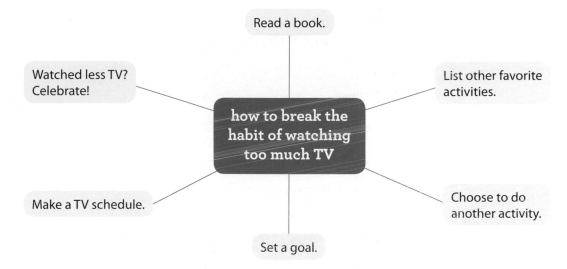

Tip Critical Thinking

In Activity A, you have to gather, or **generate**, ideas. **Generating** ideas is an important step in speaking and writing tasks. You put information together in a new way to prepare for your presentation.

PREPARE AND SPEAK

A. GATHER IDEAS Choose your topic. Then complete a graphic organizer.

1. Choose a topic from the list below or think of your own topic. Write your topic in your notebook.

- Good habits (How to start...)
- Bad habits (How to stop...)
- Personality traits (How to be more/less...)

- New skills/hobbies/sports (How to start/learn...)
- New jobs (How to become...)
- Other:

   _____

2. Complete a graphic organizer with ideas for your topic in your notebook. As an example, here is Mei Ling's graphic organizer for how to break the habit of watching too much TV.

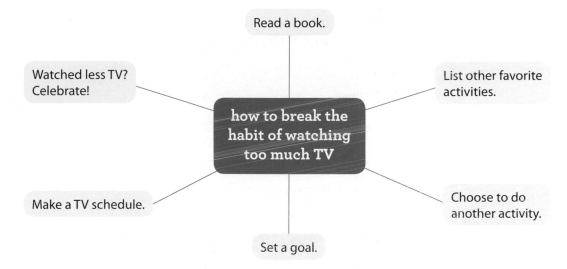

B. **ORGANIZE IDEAS** Choose an example from your notes in Activity A. In your notebook, write steps and instructions for how to make the change. Think about places where you can give advice with *be* + adjective.

C. **SPEAK** Complete the activities. Refer to the Self-Assessment checklist before you begin.

1. Work with a partner. Practice giving your instructions. Remember to check for your partner's understanding.

2. Work in a group. Take turns giving your instructions. Refer to the rubric below before you begin. Use your notes from Activity B if you need to, but make eye contact as much as possible.

CHECK AND REFLECT

A. **CHECK** Think about the Unit Assignment as you complete the Self-Assessment checklist.

Yes	No	SELF-ASSESSMENT
☐	☐	I was able to speak easily about the topic.
☐	☐	My partner/group/class understood me.
☐	☐	I used the imperative of *be* + adjective correctly.
☐	☐	I used vocabulary from the unit.
☐	☐	I checked for understanding.
☐	☐	I stressed content words in sentences.

B. **REFLECT** Discuss these questions with a partner.

What is something new you learned in this unit?

 Think about the Unit Question, "Is it ever too late to change?" Is your answer different now than when you started this unit? If yes, how is it different? Why?

Track Your Success

Circle the words you learned in this unit.

Nouns
advice 🔑
goal 🔑 AWL
habit 🔑
opportunity 🔑
progress 🔑
proverb

Verbs
accept 🔑
achieve 🔑 AWL
encourage 🔑
recommend 🔑
remain 🔑
remind 🔑

Adjectives
flexible AWL

Adverb
especially 🔑

Phrasal Verbs
stick to

Collocations
achieve a goal
change your attitude
change your mind
follow advice
give advice
make changes
make progress
set a goal

Expressions
I (totally) agree.
You're right.
I think so, too.
That's true.
Me, too.
Definitely!
I disagree.
I'm not sure I agree.
I don't think so.
I don't know if I agree.
That's not true.
I don't know about that.
Does that make sense?
Does everyone under-
   stand?
Is that clear?
Are there any questions?

🔑 Oxford 2000 keywords
AWL Academic Word List

Check (✓) the skills you learned. If you need more work on a skill, refer to the page(s) in parentheses.

LISTENING ◯	I can listen for different opinions. (p. 164)
VOCABULARY ◯	I can recognize and use verb + noun collocations. (p. 169)
GRAMMAR ◯	I can recognize and use *be* + adjective + infinitive. (p. 171)
PRONUNCIATION ◯	I can use content word stress in sentences. (p. 172)
SPEAKING ◯	I can check for listeners' understanding. (p. 173)
LEARNING OUTCOME ◯	I can deliver a presentation providing instructions on how a person can make a change in his/her life.

LISTENING	taking classification notes
VOCABULARY	idioms and expressions
GRAMMAR	*so* and *such* with adjectives
PRONUNCIATION	linking vowel sounds with /w/ or /y/
SPEAKING	expressing emotions

LEARNING OUTCOME

Use phrases for expressing emotions to describe a frightening experience.

Unit QUESTION

When is it good to be afraid?

PREVIEW THE UNIT

A Discuss these questions with your classmates.

What kinds of things make you feel afraid?

Do you enjoy the feeling of fear, for example, when you see a horror movie or ride on a fast theme-park ride?

Look at the photo. How do you think the people feel?

B Discuss the Unit Question above with your classmates.

Listen to *The Q Classroom*, Track 24 on CD 3, to hear other answers.

C These pictures show common fears many people have. Check (✓) the things you are afraid of. Then discuss your answers with a partner.

Insects and/or snakes

Speaking in public

Public transportation

Closed spaces

High places

Storms

D Ask five classmates about their worst fear from Activity C. Then ask them one more thing they are afraid of.

What are you afraid of?

Classmate's Name	Worst fear from activity	Another fear
1.		
2.		
3.		
4.		
5.		

E Work in a group and discuss the questions.

1. Do you and your classmates have the same fears? How are they the same? How are they different?

2. What is one thing a classmate is afraid of that you aren't? Do you understand this fear?

3. Do you think people learn to be afraid of things or do you think people are born that way?

LISTENING 1 | The Science of Fear

VOCABULARY

Here are some words and phrases from Listening 1. Read the definitions. Then complete each sentence with the correct word.

> **anxiety** (*noun*) a general feeling of worry or fear
> **get over** (*verb*) to become well or happy again after a difficult time or sickness
> **panic** (*verb*) to get a sudden feeling of fear that you cannot control
> **phobia** (*noun*) a very, very strong fear of something
> **protect** (*verb*) to keep somebody or something safe
> **purpose** (*noun*) the reason for something
> **strength** (*noun*) physical power
> **sweat** (*verb*) to have liquid come from your skin, often because you are hot

1. You should join a karate class. It will help you build _____ ___ _.

2. Lucia has a _____ ___ of spiders. She saw one in her bedroom last month, and now she won't sleep there anymore.

3. I get nervous when I fly. I start to ____ ____ _____, even if I'm not very hot.

4. I live alone, and sometimes I feel afraid at night. I'm happy I have a dog to _____ me.

5. My first experience with public speaking was so terrible. I don't think I will ever _____ it.

6. Many students hate taking tests. They don't understand the _____ of them, and they don't think they are necessary.

7. If there is a fire, the important thing is not to _____. Stay calm and walk, don't run, to the nearest exit.

8. A lot of people feel _____ about the future. They worry a lot about our environment.

PREVIEW LISTENING 1

The Science of Fear

You are going to listen to a conference presentation called "The Science of Fear." In this presentation, the speaker will discuss different types of fear, the body's reaction to fear, and the purpose of fear.

What do you think the speaker will say is the basic purpose of fear? Check (✓) your answer.

☐ It helps protect us from dangerous situations.

☐ It helps us feel less pain when we are hurt.

LISTEN FOR MAIN IDEAS

 CD 3
Track 25

Read the statements. Then listen to the presentation. Write *T* (true) or *F* (false).

____ 1. Fear is different from other emotions, like happiness or sadness.

____ 2. There are several different types of fear.

____ 3. Most people are afraid of flying.

____ 4. Fear causes many changes in the body.

____ 5. Fear helps protect us from danger.

____ 6. Fear is always a bad feeling.

LISTEN FOR DETAILS

CD 3
Track 26

Listen again. Circle the correct information in each sentence.

1. The situations that make us feel fear are (the same / different) for everyone.

2. One of the most common anxieties is about (money / snakes).

3. Panic is a (small / strong) type of fear.

4. People can sometimes get over (fear / phobias) with the help of a doctor.

5. Fear causes the brain to (move faster / make chemicals).

6. When we feel fear, our bodies get (warmer / colder).

7. Our bodies feel (strong and tight / weak and tired) when we feel fear.

8. Fear sometimes causes people to have amazing (dreams / strength).

Q **WHAT DO YOU THINK?**

Discuss the questions in a group.

1. In the presentation, the speaker discusses three types of fear: anxiety, panic, and phobia. Do you have these types of fears? If yes, what about?

   Anxiety: _____ _____

   Panic: _____

   Phobia: _____

2. The presenter says that sometimes people enjoy the feeling of fear such as when they watch a horror movie. Can you think of other examples? Write them in your notebook. Then discuss.

   _____ skydiving _____   _____

   ____ riding a roller coaster ____   _____

A roller coaster

Listening Skill | **Taking classification notes**

Often you need to take notes during a lecture or presentation. One way to write and organize the information is with **classification notes**. To take classification notes, write the main categories of information in the lecture or presentation. Then below each category, write the important ideas and information the speaker gives. Use numbers or bullet points (•) to help you find the important points in your notes more easily.

Tip for Success
You can prepare an outline for your classification notes before you go to a class. This will save you time.

Classification notes: The Science of Fear

Category: *Types of fear*	Category: *The effects of fear*
Ideas and information: Different types—can be mild or strong 1) Anxiety—worry about the future, money, work, personal relationships 2) Panic—sudden, strong feelings, can't think clearly 3) Phobia—strong fear of person, place, or thing—(spiders, high places, closed spaces) sometimes get over it with doctor	Ideas and information: Brain makes chemicals...

CD 3
Track 27

A. Listen to the excerpt from the presentation. Practice writing classification notes in your notebook.

CD 3
Track 28

B. Listen to the next part of the lecture and take more classification notes in your notebook.

LISTENING 2 | What Are You Afraid of?

Tip for Success

Go back and review your notes within 24 hours of taking them. Rewrite any words or sections that you can't read or that don't make sense.

VOCABULARY

Here are some words from Listening 2. Read the sentences. Circle the correct definition for each bold word.

1. Some people are afraid of snakes, but snakes don't **bother** me. I like them.
   a. to annoy or worry somebody
   b. to understand clearly

2. John is **terrified** of closed spaces. It's too scary for him to ride in elevators or cars.
   a. very happy
   b. very afraid

3. I didn't sleep much last night. I had a **nightmare**. I thought there were spiders all over me.
   a. bad dream
   b. bad job

4. Ken hates high places. He prefers to stay close to the **ground**.
   a. front of a building
   b. surface of the Earth

5. **Normal** people are not afraid to go outside. But some people are afraid to leave their houses.
   a. usual
   b. special

6. A lot of people have **negative** feelings about spiders.
   a. bad
   b. good

7. Jim loves speaking in public. He is the **ideal** person for the sales position.
   a. normal
   b. perfect

8. Public speaking can be scary at first, but after you give a few presentations, you **get used to** it.
   a. begin to feel comfortable
   b. become more afraid

PREVIEW LISTENING 2

What Are You Afraid of?

You are going to listen to a woman talking to a doctor about her phobia of high places. Do you believe it is possible to get over a phobia?

LISTEN FOR MAIN IDEAS

CD 3
Track 29

Read the statements. Then listen to the conversation and check (✓) the four reasons Marcie came to the doctor.

____ 1. She wants to stop having nightmares.

____ 2. She plans to live in a tall building.

____ 3. She wants to do more things with her friends.

____ 4. She hopes to find a new job.

____ 5. She wants to go rock climbing with her boss.

____ 6. She wants to have a normal life.

LISTEN FOR DETAILS

Listen again. Circle the correct answer.

1. How many times did Marcie visit Doctor Travis?
   a. This is her first visit.
   b. This is her second visit.
   c. She visits him often.

2. How old was Marcie when her phobia started?
   a. 10 years old
   b. 12 years old
   c. 20 years old

3. What was her nightmare about?
   a. jumping off a tall building
   b. climbing a tall building
   c. falling off a tall building

4. What makes Marcie feel afraid?
   a. the tops of tall buildings
   b. only very high places, like buildings and bridges
   c. any place above the ground

5. How does Marcie feel about her phobia?
   a. She is upset about it.
   b. She is afraid of it.
   c. She is positive about it.

6. Why didn't Marcie take the ideal job?
   a. Because the company was on the other side of town.
   b. Because she didn't like the boss of the company.
   c. Because her friends invited her rock climbing.

7. Does the doctor think Marcie can get over her phobia?
   a. No.
   b. Yes.
   c. He doesn't know.

8. According to the doctor, what can you do to get over a phobia?
   a. avoid the things that scare you
   b. look at pictures of people who have phobias
   c. stop avoiding the thing that scares you

 **WHAT DO YOU THINK?**

A. Discuss the questions in a group.

1. Do you think Marcie will be successful at getting over her phobia? Why or why not?

2. Do you know anyone with a phobia? What kind of phobia? What is that person doing to get over the phobia?

B. Think about both Listening 1 and Listening 2 as you discuss the questions.

1. What are some ways that fear can be good and bad in our lives? Write your ideas in the chart.

Ways fear can be good	Ways fear can be bad

2. Why do you think some fears are good and others are bad?

Vocabulary Skill | **Idioms and expressions**

Idioms and expressions are phrases or sentences that have a special meaning. These phrases or sentences can be difficult to understand because you cannot easily guess the meaning, even if you know all of the words. Speakers often use idioms and expressions, so it's important to learn them.

Idiom or expression	Meaning
Please, **have a seat**.	Sit down.
Go ahead, **I'm all ears**.	I'm listening carefully.

Tip for Success

Dictionaries will
often include idioms
along with the
regular definitions
of a word. They
are often labeled
as *idiom* or idm.

A. Work with a partner. Underline the idiom in each sentence. The idioms are from Listening 2.

1. When I woke up, I was sweating and <u>shaking like a leaf</u>.

2. I can't stand being up above the ground.

3. You can say that again. It really makes my life difficult.

4. So, I guess I'll just keep the job I have—even though my boss drives me crazy.

5. You may have a hard time looking at the photos at first.

6. You will get used to it before you know it.

B. Match each idiom from Activity A with the correct meaning.

a. make someone feel annoyed or angry

b. very quickly

c. unable to control your body's movement because you feel very afraid

d. have difficulty

e. don't like at all

f. you're right

____ 1. shaking like a leaf

____ 2. can't stand

____ 3. You can say that again.

____ 4. drives me crazy

____ 5. have a hard time

____ 6. before you know it

SPEAKING

Grammar | *So* and *such* with adjectives

We use *so* and *such* with adjectives to express a stronger feeling than the adjective by itself.

We usually use *so* + adjective.

I was **so scared**! = I was very scared!

We use *such* + *a/an* + adjective + singular noun.

It was **such a loud noise**! (It was a very loud noise!)

We use *such* + adjective + plural noun.

They were **such scary movies**! (They were very scary movies!)

A. Complete each sentence with *so* or *such*.

1. The spider was _____ big that I thought it was a mouse.

2. The apartment was on _____ a high floor that I couldn't live there.

3. I was _____ nervous that my knees were shaking.

4. Sun-mi is _____ afraid of snakes that she can't even look at a picture of one.

5. The rat had _____ sharp teeth that it could bite through wood.

6. I hid under my bed covers because it was _____ a bad storm.

7. Mia was _____ tired that she slept through the horror movie.

8. My sister had _____ a hard time getting used to the small elevator in her building.

B. Write sentences with *so* or *such* + the words in parentheses.

1.   I was so scared! _____
      (scared)

2. _____
      (a big snake)

3. _____
      (a scary movie)

4. _____
(afraid of public speaking)

5. _____
(worried)

6. _____
(a long flight)

7. _____
(loud)

8. _____
(an important test)

C. Take turns reading your sentences aloud with a partner.

Pronunciation	Linking vowel sounds with /w/ or /y/

CD 3
Track 31

When a word ends with a vowel sound and the next word begins with a vowel sound, we link the words with /w/ or /y/.

Linking vowel sounds with /w/

If our lips are round at the end of the first word (as with /o/ or /u/ sounds), we link another word beginning with a vowel with /w/.

Listen to these phrases.

you are   who is   go up
  w   w   w

Linking vowel sounds with /y/

If our lips are wide at the end of the first word (as with /i/, /e/, or /a/ sounds), we link another word beginning with a vowel with /y/.

Listen to these phrases.

I am   she is   we aren't
 y   y   y

A. Underline the pair of words in each sentence where the first word ends with a vowel sound, and the second word begins with a vowel sound. Then write the correct linking sound, /w/, or /y/.

<u>/w/</u> 1. Are <u>you afraid</u> of bats?

_____ 2. Why are you scared of snakes?

_____ 3. Julio is afraid of high places.

_____ 4. She always screams when she hears thunder.

_____ 5. Do you know anyone at this party?

_____ 6. She is making me nervous.

_____ 7. I don't see anyone I know here.

_____ 8. I know three other people who have a phobia of closed spaces.

 CD 3
Track 32

B. **Listen to the sentences. Check your answers. Then take turns reading the sentences aloud with a partner.**

Speaking Skill   **Expressing emotion**

Part of having a conversation is listening and responding. It's important to know *how* to respond to different types of information. It shows other people that you are listening and interested in what they are saying. Here are some phrases you can use to react to what someone tells you.

Expressing surprise	Expressing happiness	Expressing sadness
No kidding!	I'm glad to hear that.	I'm sorry to hear that.
No way!	That's wonderful.	That's terrible!
Are you serious?	Super.	How awful.

A. **Read the conversations. Complete each conversation by choosing the best expression.**

1. **A:** I'm really afraid of bears.

   B: (No kidding! / I'm glad to hear that.) I think they're beautiful animals.

2. **A:** Birds scare me. I'm always afraid they are going to land on me.

   B: Oh, I love birds. I had four birds at home, but one of them died last month.

   A: (Super. / I'm sorry to hear that.)

3. **A:** I just gave a speech to everyone in my school!

   B: I thought you were afraid of public speaking.

   A: I was afraid, but I spent a lot of time practicing with small groups and I got over my fear!

   B: (That's wonderful. / That's terrible!)

4. **A:** How is your sister?

   B: She's not doing very well.

   A: Why not?

   B: You know, she's a very nervous person. She's afraid of loud noises, and her new neighbor is a musician. He practices every day, and he's really loud!

   A: (I'm glad to hear that. / How awful.)

5. **A:** What do you think of spiders? Are you afraid of them?

   B: Yeah, I'm really afraid of spiders! I accidentally ate one once!

   A: (I'm sorry to hear that. / No way!) How did that happen?

   B: It was in my food, and I didn't see it.

B. Use the expressions from the Speaking Skill box on page 191 to complete the conversations. Different answers are possible. Then take turns reading the conversations aloud with a partner.

1. **A:** I heard a loud noise in the kitchen last night when I was home alone. It sounded like a scream. I was so scared.

   B: _____ What was it?

   A: It was just my cat! He was stuck behind the refrigerator, and he couldn't get out! He's OK now.

   B: _____

2. **A:** I saw a scary movie last month, and now I have nightmares every night.

   B: _____

   A: That's OK. The dreams gave me an idea for a story. Now I'm writing a book!

   B: _____

3. A: My company is moving its head office.

   B: _____ Where is it moving to?

   A: Well, it's going to be on the 60th floor of a building downtown. I can't work there anymore because I'm afraid of high places!

   B: _____

Unit Assignment | Tell a personal story

 In this assignment, you will tell your classmates about a time when you were afraid. You can also choose to talk about someone you know. As you prepare for your story, think about the Unit Question, "When is it good to be afraid?" and refer to the Self-Assessment checklist on page 194.

For alternative unit assignments, see the *Q: Skills for Success Teacher's Handbook*.

CONSIDER THE IDEAS

CD 3
Track 33 Listen to Margo tell her story to her friend. Then complete the information in the chart.

When and where it happened	Who was there	What happened
How I felt	**What I did**	**How the story ended**

PREPARE AND SPEAK

A. GATHER IDEAS Think of three times in your life when you felt afraid. Make brief notes in your notebook.

B. **ORGANIZE IDEAS** Choose one event from Activity A to tell a story about. Then complete the chart.

When and where did it happen?	Who was there?	What happened?

How did you feel?	What did you do?	How did the story end?

C. **SPEAK** Work in a group. Take turns telling your stories. Use the notes in your chart in Activity B to help you. Refer to the Self-Assessment checklist below before you begin.

CHECK AND REFLECT

A. **CHECK** Think about the Unit Assignment as you complete the Self-Assessment checklist.

SELF-ASSESSMENT		
Yes	No	
☐	☐	I was able to speak easily about the topic.
☐	☐	My partner/group/class understood me.
☐	☐	I used *so* and *such* with adjectives.
☐	☐	I used vocabulary from the unit.
☐	☐	I expressed surprise, happiness, and sadness.
☐	☐	I linked vowel sounds correctly.

B. **REFLECT** Discuss these questions with a partner.

What is something new you learned in this unit?

 Think about the Unit Question, "When is it good to be afraid?" Is your answer different now than when you started this unit? If yes, how is it different? Why?

Track Your Success

Circle the words you learned in this unit.

Nouns
anxiety
ground 🔑
nightmare
phobia
purpose 🔑
strength 🔑

Verbs
bother 🔑
panic
protect 🔑
sweat 🔑

Adjectives
ideal
negative 🔑 AWL
normal 🔑 AWL
terrified

Phrasal Verbs
get over

Idioms and Expressions
get used to
Have a seat.
I'm all ears.
shaking like a leaf

You can say that again.
Are you serious?
No kidding!
No way!
I'm glad to hear that.
That's wonderful.
Super.
How awful.
I'm sorry to hear that.
That's terrible!

🔑 Oxford 2000 keywords

AWL Academic Word List

Check (✓) the skills you learned. If you need more work on a skill, refer to the page(s) in parentheses.

LISTENING ●	I can take classification notes. (p. 183)
VOCABULARY ●	I can recognize and use idioms and expressions. (p. 187)
GRAMMAR ●	I can recognize and use *so* and *such* with adjectives. (p. 189)
PRONUNCIATION ●	I can link vowel sounds. (p. 190)
SPEAKING ●	I can express emotion. (p. 191)
LEARNING OUTCOME ●	I can use phrases for expressing emotions to describe a frightening experience.

Unit 1: Names

The Q Classroom Page 3

Teacher: Every unit in Q begins with a question. Your answer to the Unit Question when you start the unit can be different from your answer at the end of the unit. OK? The question for Unit 1 is "Do you like your name?" How about you, Yuna? Were you named after someone in your family?

Yuna: Yes, my aunt.

Teacher: Is your name common in Korea?

Yuna: Yes, it is.

Teacher: What about you, Sophy? Where did your name come from?

Sophy: It's not really a family name. My parents just liked it.

Teacher: Do you like it?

Sophy: Yes, I do. But people spell it wrong a lot. Or they think it's short for Sofia, but it's not.

Teacher: Do you like your name, Marcus?

Marcus: Sure. It's a great name. It was my father's and my grandfather's and my great-grandfather's.

Teacher: What does your name mean, Felix?

Felix: It means "happy." I like my name in Spanish, but I don't really like the way people say it in English.

Teacher: Oh, that's too bad. You'll have to help me pronounce it correctly.

LISTENING 1: Given Names and Nicknames
Listen for Main Ideas Page 6

Hassan: OK. Welcome to today's study group… Let's talk about the article on names. Can anyone tell me something about it?

Jim: Sure. The article is about given names and nicknames. For example, Tom is a nickname for Thomas and Liz for Elizabeth. It says that the way you say your name can give people a different **opinion** about you. For example, when I introduce myself with my given name, James, people think **differently** about me than when I use my nickname, Jim.

Emiko: Yes, the article is interesting. It also says that people connect names with a type of **personality**, like an **honest** personality.

Hassan: Can you say more about that, Emiko?

Emiko: Well, for example, if you use your given name, people think that you are honest. And using your given name also makes people feel that you are successful.

Jim: Yes, and if you use your nickname, people think you are **friendly** or **popular**.

Emiko: So, people have a different opinion of you, depending on your name.

Listen for Details Page 6

(Repeat Main Ideas track)

LISTENING SKILL: Listening for examples
A. Page 7

1. Some English names have nicknames, such as Jen or Tony.
2. In Asian countries, like Korea and Japan, names have a special meaning.
3. Some people have the same name as another family member, for example, a parent or a grandparent.
4. In Russia, some family names are very common, such as Ivanov or Petrov.

B. Page 8

Hassan: Let's talk about the article on names. Can anyone tell me something about it?

Jim: Sure. The article is about given names and nicknames—for example, Tom is a nickname for Thomas and Liz for Elizabeth. It says that the way you say your name can give people a different opinion about you. For example, when I introduce myself with my given name, James, people think differently about me than when I use my nickname, Jim.

Emiko: Yes, the article is interesting. It also says that people connect names with a type of personality, like an honest personality.

Hassan: Can you say more about that, Emiko?

Emiko: Well, for example, if you use your given name, people think that you are honest, And using your given name also makes people feel that you are successful.

Jim: Yes, and if you use your nickname, people think you are friendly or popular.

Emiko: So, people have a different opinion of you, depending on your name.

LISTENING 2: Stage Names
Listen for Main Ideas Page 10

Host: Welcome to Star Talk. We're here with Hollywood reporter, Stella Skye, to talk about stage names—names stars take when they become **famous**. Stella, why do some singers and actors change their names?

Stella: Well, one reason is because their real names are too **ordinary**. Stars want people to remember their names. For example, do you know the name Richard Starkey?

Host: No, I don't. Who is he?

Stella: That's the real name of Beatles drummer, Ringo Starr. His stage name is much more interesting. No one will forget it.

Host: Yes, that's true. I guess stars want an **unusual** name—a name no one else has.

Stella: Right. And another reason some stars change their names is that they want a name that is easy to **pronounce** in English. As a child, Bruce Lee had a Chinese name, Lee Zhen Fan. When he became an international star, he needed a name that people from around the world could say.

Host: Hmm. Yes, I see. So, how do celebrities **choose** their stage names?

Stella: Well, some choose a name that's **similar** to their real name. Other celebrities choose a nickname, for example, singer and actor

Miley Cyrus uses a nickname her father gave her when she was a child. He called her "Smiley Miley."

Host: That's cute. Well, what advice would you give to someone who wanted to choose a stage name?

Stella: Hmm. I guess the most important thing is to choose a name that *you* like—something you will be able to live with for the rest of your life.

Host: Right. Good advice. Well, Stella, thank you for coming on the show today. We'll see you later, everybody. Join us next time for…

Listen for Details Page 11

(Repeat Main Ideas track)

PRONUNCIATION: Intonation in *yes/no* and information questions
Examples Page 18

Are you Mark Johnson? [rising intonation]

Does she have a stage name? [rising intonation]

Examples Page 18

What is your family name? [falling intonation]

Why do people change their names? [falling intonation]

A. Page 18

1. What is your family name? [falling intonation]

2. Do you have a nickname? [rising intonation]

3. Where are you from? [falling intonation]

4. Where do you live now? [falling intonation]

5. Is your family name common? [rising intonation]

6. Do you have any brothers? [rising intonation]

7. Why do you like your name? [falling intonation]

8. Does it rain a lot where you come from? [rising intonation]

Unit 2: Work

The Q Classroom Page 25

Teacher: The question for Unit 2 is "How can you find a good job?" What are some ways people find jobs? Yuna?

Yuna: Internet, friends, family, help-wanted signs.

Teacher: That's right. Which one is the best way to find a job, Marcus?

Marcus: Maybe friends. You can walk in to a business or apply online, but they don't know who you are. It's harder to get hired.

Teacher: Do you agree, Sophy? Is it hard to get a job if you don't know anyone at the company?

Sophy: Sometimes. But it doesn't have to be a friend. Someone you know from school or a friend of a friend can help you find a good job. It's important to tell everyone that you're looking for work.

Teacher: What do you think, Felix? How do you find a good job?

Felix: I think you can get a good job by working your way up. You know, you start at a company in an entry-level position. After you show them how good you are, you get a better-paying, more interesting job.

LISTENING 1: Looking for a Job
Listen for Main Ideas Page 28

Sarah: Hmm… Interesting…

Sehoon: What are you doing, Sarah?

Sarah: Oh, hi, Sehoon. I'm looking at this company's website. I want to work there this summer.

Sehoon: Hmm. Braxton Books. That's the big bookstore downtown, right?

Sarah: Right. I'm reading all about the company. I want to see what kind of summer jobs they have… Hey, look at this. There's a link on the website for jobs.

Sehoon: "**Careers** at Braxton Books." Hmm. Click on it. Let's see what it says.

Sarah: OK.

Sehoon: Oh, look, click on this, it's a Web video with information about jobs. Let's watch it.

1. **Speaker:** Thank you for your interest in careers at Braxton Books. Our company began ten years ago, and it is still growing. We opened our first store in Chicago in 1998. We had 25 **employees** then. Today we have over 200 stores and 6,000 employees around the world. In 2009, we started our e-book business. It was a big success. We plan to continue growing our online library. We hope you'll join our team and share our success.

2. **Speaker:** Are you looking for an interesting job? Braxton Books has job openings for great people. Right now we have positions for salespeople and Web designers. If you'd like to join our team, please listen to the **requirements** for each job.

3. **Speaker:** Here are the requirements for salespeople: You need one to two years of experience in sales. We also require some **basic** computer skills. Our stores are very busy, so you must be **organized**. Finally, you must be friendly and enjoy working with people on a team.

   Braxton Books needs Web designers for our e-book department. Here are the requirements for the position. You must have at least five years of experience in Web design and excellent computer skills with different computer systems. We prefer people with a college **degree** in Web design. We are looking for organized people who have new and interesting ideas.

4. **Speaker:** If you are interested in one of these jobs, please come to one of our stores and complete an **application**, or print the application from our website and bring it with you to one of our stores. If you meet our requirements, we will contact you for an **interview**. Thank you again for your interest in working at Braxton Books.

   Sarah: Wow. It sounds like a great place to work.

   Sehoon: It sure does! Well, what are you waiting for? Print the application!

Listen for Details Page 28

Speaker: Here are the requirements for salespeople: You need one to two years of experience in sales. We also require some basic computer skills. Our stores are very busy, so you must be organized. Finally, you must be friendly and enjoy working with people on a team.

Braxton Books needs Web designers for our e-book department. Here are the requirements for the position. You must have at least five years of experience in Web design and excellent computer skills with different computer systems. We prefer people with a college degree in Web design. We are looking for organized people who have new and interesting ideas.

LISTENING SKILL: Listening for key words and phrases
Page 29

Sarah: Hmm… Interesting…

Sehoon: What are you doing, Sarah?

Sarah: Oh, hi, Sehoon. I'm looking at this company's website. I want to work there this summer.

Sehoon: Hmm. Braxton Books. That's the big bookstore downtown, right?

Sarah: Right. I'm reading all about the company. I want to see what kind of summer jobs they have… Hey, look at this. There's a link on the website for jobs.

Sehoon: "Careers at Braxton Books." Hmm. Click on it. Let's see what it says.

Sarah: OK.

Sehoon: Oh, look, click on this, it's a Web video with information about jobs. Let's watch it.

A. Page 29

1. **Speaker:** Thank you for your interest in careers at Braxton Books. Our company began ten years ago, and it is still growing. We opened our first store in Chicago in 1998. We had 25 employees then. Today we have over 200 stores and 6,000 employees around the world. In 2009, we started our e-book business. It was a big success. We plan to continue growing our online library. We hope you'll join our team and share our success.

2. **Speaker:** Are you looking for an interesting job? Braxton Books has job openings for great people. Right now we have positions for salespeople and Web designers. If you'd like to join our team, please listen to the requirements for each job.

3. **Speaker:** Here are the requirements for salespeople: You need one to two years of experience in sales. We also require some basic computer skills. Our stores are very busy, so you must be organized. Finally, you must be friendly and enjoy working with people on a team.

   Braxton Books needs Web designers for our e-book department. Here are the requirements for the position. You must have at least five years of experience in Web design and excellent computer skills with different computer systems. We prefer people with a college degree in Web design. We are looking for organized people who have new and interesting ideas.

4. **Speaker:** If you are interested in one of these jobs, please come to one of our stores and complete an application, or print the application from our website and bring it with you to one of our stores. If you meet our requirements, we will contact you for an interview. Thank you again for your interest in working at Braxton Books.

B. Page 30

(Repeat Listening Skill A track)

LISTENING 2: The Right Person for the Job
Listen for Main Ideas Page 31

1. **Margaret:** Hello, I'm Margaret Williamson. I'm the **manager** of New World Design.

Tom: Hi, I'm Tom. It's nice to meet you, Ms. Williamson.

Margaret: Well, let's get started. Please sit down, Tom.… OK. Can you tell me a little about yourself?

Tom: Sure. I came to New York a few months ago from Chicago. I went to Chicago School of Design.

Margaret: Yes, I saw that on your **resume**. Yes, here it is. You **graduated** last May. What did you study there?

Tom: I'm sorry. I didn't catch that. Could you say that again, please?

Margaret: Sure. What was your **major** in college?

Tom: Well, I got my degree in art. I took a lot of computer classes, too. I wanted to use my art and computer skills. That's why I want a career in Web design.

Margaret: I see… And do you have any experience in **advertising**?

Tom: Do you mean work experience… in a company?

Margaret: Yes. You need two years of experience for this job.

Tom: No, I'm sorry, I don't. I worked at a convenience store in college, and when I was in high school, I worked in a restaurant…

2. **Margaret:** Hi, you must be Ms. Lopez. I'm Margaret Williamson.

Wendy: Good afternoon, Ms. Williamson. It's nice to meet you. Please call me Wendy.

Margaret: OK, Wendy. Please have a seat. Let's see… your resume says you have some experience in advertising. Tell me about that. Did you like it?

Wendy: Oh, yes. It was a great experience. I worked in a small advertising company last summer. I really enjoyed it. I was an **assistant** in the office. I didn't do much Web design work—only a little. But I learned a lot from my co-workers. I'm excited to learn more about it.

Margaret: OK, that's excellent, Wendy. Did you study art or computers in college?

Wendy: No. My major was English. I didn't have a lot of time for other classes.

Margaret: All right. Can you tell me what makes you the right person for this job?

Wendy: Do you mean my skills?

Margaret: Yes, your skills and your personality.

Wendy: Well, I'm organized and friendly, and I think I have a lot of new and different ideas. I also enjoy working with others on team projects.

Margaret: Uh huh. Do you have any questions about our company or about the position?

Wendy: Yes, I do have a few questions. I saw on your website that the company…

Listen for Details Page 31

(Repeat Main Ideas track)

PRONUNCIATION: Simple past –ed.
Page 37

enjoy	enjoyed	help	helped
study	studied	wash	washed
learn	learned	graduate	graduated

laugh laughed   end ended

work worked

B. Page 37

Column 1, /t/	Column 2, /d/	Column 3, /əd/
liked	changed	completed
looked	preferred	needed
stopped	required	waited
walked	studied	wanted

SPEAKING SKILL: Asking for repetition and clarification
A. Page 39

Margaret: Well, let's get started. Please sit down, Tom…. OK. Can you tell me a little about yourself?

Tom: Sure. I came to New York a few months ago from Chicago. I went to Chicago School of Design.

Margaret: Yes, I saw that on your resume. Yes, here it is. You graduated last May. What did you study there?

Tom: I'm sorry. I didn't catch that. Could you say that again, please?

Margaret: Sure. What was your major in college?

Tom: Well, I got my degree in art. I took a lot of computer classes, too. I wanted to use my art and computer skills. That's why I want a career in Web design.

Margaret: I see…And do you have any experience in advertising?

Tom: Do you mean work experience… in a company?

Margaret: Yes. You need two years of experience for this job.

B. Page 39

1. **Michael:** Hello?

   Susan: Hello, is this Michael Lu?

   Michael: Yes, it is.

   Susan: Oh, hi, Michael. It's Susan Barden from All-Tech Computers.
   Thank you for coming to the interview this morning. I forgot to ask you about…

   Michael: Hello… ? I'm sorry. I didn't catch that.

2. **Interviewer:** Great. OK, thanks. And can you tell me a little about your experience in Australia? I saw on your resume that you…

   Linda: I'm sorry. Could you say that again, please?

3. **Min-Hee:** Hey, Jared! How are you doing?

   Jared: Oh, hi, Min-Hee. I'm great! I just found out that…

   Min-Hee: Sorry, Jared. Could you repeat that?

4. **Amber:** What do you plan to do after you graduate, Seth?

   Seth: Well, I had a meeting with the manager of New World Designs last week.

   Amber: A meeting? Do you mean an interview?

Unit 3: Long Distance

The Q Classroom Page 45

Teacher: Here we are at Unit 3. The Unit Question is "Why do we study other cultures?" Marcus, why do you think we study other cultures?

Marcus: Well, people everywhere are so different. Different food, different customs, different beliefs.

Teacher: Yes, that's true. Yuna, do you like to study other cultures?

Yuna: Yes. It's very interesting.

Teacher: So other cultures are definitely interesting, but that's not the only reason we study them. Why else do we study other cultures, Felix?

Felix: We can learn from other cultures. We learn new ways to do things. And we also learn about new kinds of food. That's very important!

Teacher: I agree with you there! We learn new ways to do things. What do you think, Sophy? Why else do we study other cultures?

Sophy: Well, we don't just learn about our differences. We also learn about what makes us all the same. That helps us understand and accept each other. This helps us live together peacefully.

LISTENING 1: International Advertising
Listen for Main Ideas Page 48

Professor: Good afternoon, class. Our topic today is **international** advertising—how companies sell products in different countries. I'll talk about the **difficulties** of advertising in different cultures.

These days, many companies are international. Most large companies sell their products around the world, and many small companies sell their products on websites. But companies can have problems when they advertise products in other countries.

Sometimes the problem is a language **mistake**. A product name or an advertisement can have a funny or strange meaning in another language. For example, a few years ago, a large international computer company named its new product Vista. Later, the company learned that the word "vista" means *chicken* in some eastern European languages. The company didn't change the name of its product. But the example shows that it's important to think about language in international advertising.

Another problem is color. Colors have different meanings in different cultures. For example, the color red means good luck in many countries, so it's usually good to use red in advertisements. The color blue usually has a **positive** meaning also. But white means **death** in some parts of Asia, and black means death in North America. As you can see, it's important for companies to know the meaning of colors in the country where they are selling their products.

International **customs** are another difficulty in advertising. As you know, different cultures sometimes have very different ideas about things. Companies should learn the customs of the countries where they sell their products. Then they can **avoid** mistakes like this one by an international telephone company. The company made a TV advertisement for the Middle East. It showed a businessman talking on the phone with his feet up on his desk. The problem was, in the Middle East, it's not polite to show the **bottom** of your shoes. The company lost a lot of money and had to make a new advertisement.

Listen for Details Page 48

(Repeat Main Ideas track)

LISTENING SKILL: Taking notes in a T-chart
A. Page 50

Another problem is color. Colors have different meanings in different cultures. For example, the color red means good luck in many countries, so it's usually good to use red in advertisements. The color blue usually has a positive meaning also. But white means death in some parts of Asia, and black means death in North America. As you can see, it's important for companies to know the meaning of colors in the country where they are selling their products.

B. Page 50

International companies should also learn about numbers in different cultures. Some numbers can be good in one culture and bad in another culture. In some languages in Asia, the number four sounds like the word for "death," so it's not a good number for advertising. For example, a sports company wanted to sell golf balls in Korea, but the company made a mistake. It put four balls in each package, and no one in Korea bought them.

LISTENING 2: Cultural Problems
Listen for Main Ideas Page 52

1. Joao from Brazil
   Joao: When I came to the United States to study, a lot of things were different. The language, my classes at the university… I knew about those cultural differences. But one day, I went to the university bookstore to buy books for my history class. There was another student standing in front of the shelf. I stood next to her and started to look for my book. Then she looked very **upset** and said, "Excuse me!" and moved away. I didn't know what was wrong. I was **confused**. I learned later that you shouldn't stand very close to other people in the U.S. It's **rude** to stand too close.

2. Tanya from Russia
   Tanya: Last summer, my company sent me to work for two months at our head office in Toronto. It was a great experience. My Canadian co-workers were really friendly, and I learned a lot. There was one funny thing that happened. When it was time for me to leave, my co-workers had a goodbye party for me. They gave me some very nice gifts… and they gave me flowers—six flowers. In Russia, it's OK to give an odd number of flowers, for example, one, three, five… But you shouldn't give two, four, or six flowers. We only do that when a person **dies**. I wasn't really **offended**. My co-workers didn't know our custom, but some other Russians may feel angry or upset at this.

3. Rick from the U.S.
   Rick: My friend Hiro got married last summer in Japan, and he **invited** me to the **wedding**. It was a great trip. I really enjoyed meeting Hiro's family and the other guests at the wedding. Many people gave me business cards. I was a little surprised. In the U.S., we only use cards for business, so I didn't bring mine. I just took the Japanese people's business cards and put them in my pocket. After the wedding, I learned that it's not polite to do that. You should always take the cards with two hands and read them **carefully**. I only used one hand, and I didn't read them at all!

Listen for Details Page 52

(Repeat Main Ideas track)

VOCABULARY SKILL: Words in context
A. Page 54

1. Last summer, I stayed in Australia. It was my first time away from home for such a long time. In the beginning, I felt really <u>depressed</u>. I didn't know I would miss my family so much.

2. The first few weeks were <u>tough</u>. I often felt lonely, and I wanted to go home.

3. But the family I lived with was great. They were very kind and <u>considerate</u>.

4. They taught me about Australian culture and customs. And they <u>treated</u> me like a member of the family. That really helped me feel better.

5. After a few weeks, I didn't miss home so much. I felt happy and <u>optimistic</u> again. In fact, I didn't want to come home at the end of the summer!

B. Page 54

(Repeat Vocabulary Skill A track)

GRAMMAR: Part 1. *Should* and *shouldn't*
A. Page 55

1. In India, you shouldn't use your left hand to eat.
2. In Thailand, you shouldn't touch a person on the head.
3. In the U.S., you should look at people's eyes when you speak to them.
4. In France, when you visit someone's home, you should bring a gift.
5. In Saudi Arabia, you shouldn't say *no* when someone offers you something to eat or drink.
6. In Colombia, you should avoid giving marigolds—a yellow flower—as a gift.

GRAMMAR: Part 2. *It's* + adjective + infinitive
A. Page 56

1. There was another student standing in front of the shelf. I stood next to her and started to look for my book. Then she looked very upset and said, "Excuse me!" and moved away. I didn't know what was wrong. I was confused. I learned later that you shouldn't stand very close to other people in the U.S. It's rude to stand too close.

2. They gave me some very nice gifts… and they gave me flowers—six flowers. In Russia, it's OK to give an odd number of flowers, for example, one, three, five… But you shouldn't give two, four, or six flowers. We only do that when a person dies.

3. I was a little surprised. In the U.S., we only use cards for business, so I didn't bring mine. I just took the Japanese people's business cards and put them in my pocket. After the wedding, I learned that it's not polite to do that. You should always take the cards with two hands and read them carefully. I only used one hand, and I didn't read them at all!

PRONUNCIATION: The schwa /ə/ sound
Page 57

avoid   cultural   custom   international   problem

A. Page 57

1. avoid	5. personality
2. bottom	6. positive
3. considerate	7. similar
4. mistake	8. telephone

Unit 4: Positive Thinking

The Q Classroom Page 65

Teacher: The Unit 4 Question is "What makes a happy ending?" What do you think, Yuna? Can you think of a story with a happy ending?

Yuna: Sure. My parents worked in the same company, and they met there. Then they fell in love and got married. That's a happy ending.

Teacher: Do you agree, Sophy? Does that sound like a happy ending to you?

Sophy: Yeah. A lot of movies and books have stories about people meeting and falling in love. Most movies have happy endings, I think.

Teacher: Marcus? What do you think?

Marcus: Well, sometimes a happy ending can come from something bad.

Teacher: Can you say more about that, Marcus?

Marcus: Well, for example, my friend Alex missed his train one morning, so he had to take the bus. The bus is slow, and he was worried because he didn't want to be late for school. Later, he heard that the train broke down. People were stuck on the train for three hours! So, I think that was a happy ending for him.

LISTENING 1: A Bad Situation with a Happy Ending
Listen for Main Ideas   Page 68

Speaker: This is a true story with an **amazing** happy ending.

In 1985, British mountain climbers named Joe Simpson and Simon Yates went to the Andes Mountains in Peru. They finished a very difficult climb to the top of a high point called Siula Grande. Then they started the long trip back down the mountain to their **camp**. The two climbers were still near the top of the mountain, when **suddenly**, Joe Simpson fell and broke his leg. He could not walk or climb.

The two climbers thought about what to do. They had a very long rope. Simon used the rope to slowly lower Joe down the mountainside. This plan worked at first.

Then suddenly, Simon felt a heavy weight on the end of the rope, and he knew something happened to Joe. He called to Joe but heard nothing. Simon didn't know what to do.

On the other end of the rope, Joe fell over the side of the mountain. He could not climb back up because of his **painful** broken leg.

Simon could not pull Joe back up, so he made a very difficult choice. He cut the rope.

When Simon cut the rope, Joe fell. He fell far, far down into a very deep **hole** in the ice. Joe thought there was only ice below him, and he prepared to die. But something amazing happened. He didn't fall on ice. He fell on a soft place in the snow. Joe didn't die. Even after that long fall, he was still **alive**!

Joe had no food or water. He drank a little water from the ice all around him. He thought he might die from the **effects** of the cold and wind. For three days, he pulled his body across the ice and snow, until he found an opening in the side of the ice. He climbed out, and he knew where he was—only a short **distance** from the camp! Joe arrived at the camp to find Simon and another member of their team just a few hours before they planned to leave the camp.

Listen for Details   Page 68

(Repeat Main Ideas track)

LISTENING SKILL: Using information questions to understand a story
A. Page 69

(Repeat Main Ideas track)

B. Page 70

News Announcer: In other news today, a 65-year-old Australian woman is in the hospital after a kangaroo attack. Mary Nelson lives on a farm outside of Sydney. Yesterday afternoon at around three p.m., she went outside to check on her horses. That's when she saw the two-meter-tall kangaroo. The kangaroo jumped on Mrs. Nelson, who fell down and was unable to get up. Luckily Mrs. Nelson's favorite horse ran to help its owner, jumping over the fence and chasing away the kangaroo. Mrs. Nelson says it's amazing she is still alive, and she thanks her horse.

LISTENING 2: Make Your Own Happy Ending
Listen for Main Ideas   Page 71

Interviewer: We're talking with Ellen Sharpe, author of the new book *Make Your Own Happy Ending*. Ellen, tell us about the book.

Sharpe: Sure… Well, first I'll tell you a little bit about me. When I was younger, I was always unhappy. I wanted more money, more friends, a better job, nicer clothes… I saw people who had a lot things, and I thought they were happy. I didn't appreciate my life.

Interviewer: Uh-huh. I see. So, how did you become an **expert** on happiness?

Sharpe: Well, about five years ago, something happened that **completely** changed me.

Interviewer: Really? What happened?

Sharpe: I was driving to work one morning. I was driving pretty fast because I was late for work. I looked down for my cell phone to call my boss and tell her I was late. Suddenly, my car went off the road. I don't **remember** everything, but I woke up in the hospital.

Interviewer: Oh, no. How awful! Did you **get hurt** badly?

Sharpe: Yes. I broke several bones, and I had to stay in the hospital for two months.

Interviewer: Oh, I'm sorry to hear that.

Sharpe: Well, yes, the **accident** was pretty bad… But when I was in the hospital, so many friends sent cards and flowers and visited. My parents and my brother came to visit me every day. Every time I saw them, I felt happy. They were all there when I really needed them.

Interviewer: Wow! It sounds like this experience really changed your **attitude**.

Sharpe: Yes. I learned an important lesson… I started to **appreciate** the positive things in my life—my family, my friends, even my job— and I stopped thinking about the other things I wanted.

Interviewer: Wonderful. So, what advice do you give people in *Make Your Own Happy Ending*?

Sharpe: Well, in the book, I tell people that there really is no **secret** to happiness. We can all learn to be happy. It's all about your attitude. We just need to remember and appreciate the good things in our lives. That's what the book is about. I want to help other people be happy, too.

Interviewer: Mm hmm. I see. That's great advice, Ellen. Thanks a lot for joining us today. And you can pick up Ellen's book at your local bookstore.

Sharpe: Happy to be here! And thank *you*.

Listen for Details   Page 71

(Repeat Main Ideas track)

GRAMMAR: *because* and *so*

B. Page 74

1. **A:** Why weren't you in class this morning?

   B: Well, I woke up late, so I missed the train. Then I had to go back home because I forgot all my books!

   A: That's terrible.

2. **A:** My little brother is a really good student.

   B: Why do you say that?

   A: Well, he's really smart, so he always gets good grades.

   B: Hmm. Maybe he gets good grades because he studies hard.

3. **A:** Hi, Joe. How was your vacation?

   B: Not very good.

   A: Oh, no. Why not?

   B: Our flight was late because there was a big storm. Then our hotel was full, so we didn't have a place to sleep.

   A: Wow! I'm sorry to hear that.

PRONUNCIATION: Syllables and syllable stress

Page 75

one syllable	two syllables
pain	painful [PAIN-ful]
camp	secret [SE-cret]

three syllables	four syllables
amazing [a-MA-zing]	appreciate [ap-PRE-ci-ate]
completely [com-PLETE-ly]	effectively [ef-FEC-tive-ly]

painful, amazing, appreciate

A. Page 76

1. alive
2. amazingly
3. distance
4. effective
5. hurt
6. happily
7. remember
8. suddenly

B. Page 76

1. hospital [HOS-pit-al]
2. completely [com-PLETE-ly]
3. secret [SE-cret]
4. effectively [ef-FEC-tive-ly]
5. suddenly [SUDD-en-ly]
6. attitude [AT-ti-tude]
7. control [con-TROL]
8. unhappy [un-HAP-py]

SPEAKING SKILL: Responding in a conversation

A. Page 77

1. **Ellen:** I saw people who had a lot of things, and I thought they were happy. I didn't appreciate my life.

   Interviewer: Uh-huh. I see. So, how did you become an expert on happiness?

2. **Ellen:** Well, about five years ago, something happened that completely changed me.

   Interviewer: Really? What happened?

3. **Ellen:** I don't remember everything, but I woke up in the hospital.

   Interviewer: Oh, no. How awful!

4. **Ellen:** My parents and my brother came to visit me every day. Every time I saw them, I felt happy. They were all there when I really needed them.

5. **Interviewer:** Wow! It sounds like this experience really changed your attitude.

   Ellen: That's what the book is about. I want to help other people be happy, too.

   Interviewer: Mm hmm. I see. That's great advice, Ellen.

UNIT ASSIGNMENT: Consider the Ideas

Page 78

Diego: So, Yuko, do you have a story with a happy ending?

Yuko: Well, I'm happy because I have a great job.

Diego: Uh-huh. I see. What do you do?

Yuko: I'm a nurse… It's funny. I like to travel, so I wanted to be a flight attendant—not a nurse.

Diego: So what happened?

Yuko: Well, actually, one day, I was going to an interview to be a flight attendant. I was on the bus, and it stopped suddenly. I fell and broke my arm.

Diego: Oh, no. How awful!

Yuko: I went to the hospital and saw the nurses helping everyone. And I just decided: I want to be a nurse. So I went to school, and now I work in a hospital!

Diego: Wow! That's amazing

Yuko: How about you, Diego? Do you have a story with a happy ending?

Diego: Uh, yeah. I failed a math test.

Yuko: Really? That doesn't sound very happy.

Diego: Well, at first, it wasn't. I wasn't doing well in math class. I had a bad attitude. But my parents found a great math tutor for me.

Yuko: Mm hmm.

Diego: He helped me a lot. I studied hard, and my grades got better.

Yuko: Really? That's great.

Diego: Yes. And because I got good grades, I got into a good university. And when I graduate next month, I'm going to work for a software company!

Yuko: Congratulations! That *is* a happy ending.

Unit 5: Vacation Time

The Q Classroom Page 83

Teacher: The Unit 5 Question is "What is the best kind of vacation?" What are some different kinds of vacations? Marcus?

Marcus: There are relaxing vacations, like going to the beach. There are tourism vacations, where you see sites and go to museums. There are nature vacations, where you go camping or fishing.

Teacher: Yuna, which do you think is the best kind of vacation?

Yuna: Relaxing. I like to go to the beach.

Teacher: What do you think, Sophy? What's the best kind of vacation?

Sophy: For me it's a tourism vacation. I like to visit new cities, especially in other countries, and learn about other cultures. I like to see famous art too.

Teacher: How about you, Felix? What do you think is the best kind of vacation?

Felix: Hmm. I think the best kind of vacation is something unusual, like going to Africa or seeing polar bears in the Arctic. I don't want to relax on vacation. I want to see something really different from what I see every day.

LISTENING 1: Places in Danger
Listen for Main Ideas Page 86

Speaker 1: Every year, millions of people visit famous places around the world. Tourism can be good. **Tourists** spend money. This helps **local** businesses and makes jobs for local people. But tourists can also cause problems. What are the effects of having tourists, and what are people doing to help?

Speaker 2: This is the Taj Mahal in India.

The Taj Mahal was built in 1632 by the leader of India. He built the amazing white building for his wife after she died. It took 20,000 workers and many years to finish the building. Each year, over three million tourists visit this amazing white building. Because of the **pollution** from tourist cars and buses, the building started to change color. The beautiful white stone became darker. For this reason, today only bicycles or **electric** cars can go near the building.

Speaker 1: Here we are at the Galapagos Islands off the coast of Ecuador.

The Galapagos Islands are in the Pacific Ocean near South America. The 19 main islands are home to thousands of plants and animals. About 175,000 tourists visit the islands every year. They come on planes or boats from many different places. And these planes and boats sometimes carry **insects** that don't belong in the Galapagos Islands. This is **dangerous** for the local plants and animals. Now airlines must spray visitors' clothing and bags with a special liquid to kill any insects before they get off the plane or boat.

Speaker 2: Next we visit the Great Pyramid of Giza in Egypt.

The Great Pyramid is 4,500 years old. It is 137 meters high. Workers used over two million stones to build the pyramid. Because the pyramid is very, very old, parts of it are beginning to break. Driving cars and tour buses near the pyramid is dangerous. This can **shake** the ground under the pyramid and **destroy** this amazing tourist site. Today, tourists have to park their cars far away and walk to the pyramids.

Listen for Details Page 87

(Repeat Main Ideas track)

LISTENING SKILL: Understanding numbers and dates
Page 87

Examples

fourteen [four-TEEN]	seventeen [seven-TEEN]
forty [FOR-ty]	seventy [SEVEN-ty]
fifteen [fif-TEEN]	eighteen [eight-TEEN]
fifty [FIF-ty]	eighty [EIGHT-ty]
sixteen [six-TEEN]	nineteen [nine-TEEN]
sixty [SIX-ty]	ninety [NINE-ty]

Examples Page 88

four hundred fifty-three
three thousand two hundred twenty-seven
fifteen thousand six hundred nine
two hundred seventy-five thousand
eight million two hundred fifty thousand

Examples Page 88

seventeen hundred
eighteen oh nine
nineteen eighty-nine
twenty eleven / two thousand eleven

A. Page 88

1. The Taj Mahal was built in 1632 by the leader of India. He built the amazing white building for his wife after she died. It took 20,000 workers and many years to finish the building. Each year, over three million tourists visit this amazing white building.

2. The Galapagos Islands are in the Pacific Ocean near South America. The 19 main islands are home to thousands of plants and animals. About 175,000 tourists visit the islands every year.

3. The Great Pyramid is 4,500 years old. It is 137 meters high. Workers used over two million stones to build the pyramid.

B. Page 89

1. Mt. Everest is 8,850 meters high.
2. The Eiffel Tower in Paris was built in 1889.
3. Burj Khalifa, the tallest building in the world, is 818 meters tall.
4. The population of New York City is about 8,300,000.
5. Only 300 tourists are allowed inside the Great Pyramid every day.
6. The Colosseum in Rome, Italy, was built around the year AD 70.
7. There are 7,107 islands in the Philippines.
8. Angel Falls in Venezuela is the world's tallest waterfall. It's 979 meters tall.

LISTENING 2: A Helpful Vacation
Listen for Main Ideas Page 91

Lisa: Good evening. Thank you all for coming. I'm happy that you're interested in our travel tour for **volunteers** to Cusco, Peru. Traveling and working as a volunteer is a wonderful experience, and I'm sure you're going to enjoy it. OK. Let's get started. First, I'm going to give you some information about the trip.

Cusco is a **pretty** city with a **population** of about 350,000. It's near the Andes Mountains. It's about three hours by train to Machu Picchu, the **ancient** Inca city.

Female student: Wow. Can we go there?

Lisa: Yes, at the end of the first week we are going to visit Machu Picchu. Our trip is four weeks—from June 13th to July 5th. The first two weeks will **prepare** you for your volunteer work. You're going to study Spanish and learn about the culture of Peru. Are there any questions about that?

Male Student: Yes, where are we going to stay?

Lisa: You're all going to live with local families. We have wonderful host families. You're going to eat meals with them, speak Spanish with them, and help them around the house—just like a member of the family.

Female student: What kind of volunteer work are we going to do?

Lisa: On this trip, we're going to help **repair** a local school. This school is very old, and many classrooms need repairs. We're going to put in new windows, paint the classrooms, and make it a better place for the children who study there.

Male Student: Can we meet the children?

Lisa: Yes, in fact, part of the volunteer work is teaching at the school. You're going to work with the teachers and help them with anything

...eed. You may teach English, help with art or music lessons, or
...ports or games.

...le student: That sounds great.

...Yes, most volunteers say this is the most **enjoyable** part of the
...When they see the children's happy faces, they know the positive
...cts of their work.

...ten for Details Page 92

(...epeat Main Ideas track)

...RAMMAR: *Be going to*
Page 96

1. **Female:** What are you going to do in China?

   Male: I'm going to do volunteer work in Shanghai.

2. **Female:** Where are we going to stay?

   Male: You're going to live with a local family.

3. **Female:** Can we go to the Great Pyramid today?

   Male: No, we're going to go shopping.

4. **Female:** How long is your trip?

   Male: We're going to return on May 16th.

5. **Female:** Is John going to take a vacation this year?

   Male: Yes, he's going to go to Hawaii.

PRONUNCIATION: Reduction of *be going to*
Page 97

1. We're going to visit Italy next year.

   We're going to [gonna] visit Italy next year.

2. She isn't going to come with us.

   She isn't going to [gonna] come with us.

3. I'm going to stay with a family in Madrid.

   I'm going to [gonna] stay with a family in Madrid.

4. They aren't going to join a tour.

   They aren't going to [gonna] join a tour.

UNIT ASSIGNMENT: Consider the Ideas

A. Page 99

Doug: Hello, everyone. I'm Doug, and this is Lisa. We're going to tell
you about our tree-planting tour to Nepal. Let's start with the tour
schedule. This is a 14-day tour. We're going to leave on March 9th
and come back on March 22nd. Now let's move on to lodging. In
Kathmandu, we're going to stay in a nice Western-style hotel for a few
days. When we go on our hike, we're going to camp in tents. OK. Now
Lisa is going to tell you about the activities we're going to do.

Lisa: Thanks, Doug. We're going to spend four days hiking and
camping in the Himalayas. We will learn about the plants and animals
in the mountains. On day nine of the tour, we are going to arrive at a
small village called Sirendanda. We'll spend three days planting trees
there with the local people. Next, I'm going to talk about the food.
You're going to try some local food. Meat dishes are popular, but if you
don't eat meat, the rice curry with fresh vegetables is wonderful. Doug
is going to take over.

Doug: To wrap up, I'm going to tell you about the cost. The trip costs
$2,700 dollars.

That price includes hotel and all meals…

B. Page 99

(Repeat Consider the Ideas, A.)

Unit 6: Laughter

The Q Classroom Page 103

Teacher: The Unit Question for Unit 6 is "Who makes you laugh?"
How about you, Yuna? Do like comedies on TV?

Yuna: Yes, I love them.

Teacher: Do you think American comedies or Korean comedies are
funnier?

Yuna: Korean.

Teacher: How about you, Marcus? Who makes you laugh?

Marcus: I don't like TV comedies, but I love live comedians. I like to
listen to people tell jokes. Also, I'm very funny myself.

Teacher: [laughs] That's true. You are pretty funny. Sophy, who makes
you laugh? Besides Marcus.

Sophy: I think my best friend makes me laugh. We understand each
other so well. Lots of times we laugh at things that no one else thinks
are funny.

Teacher: What do you think, Felix? Why are some things funny to
one person but not to another?

Felix: Well, you need to understand the joke. Some English-speaking
comedians aren't funny to me. It's like listening to Sophy's jokes with
her friend—I don't understand it, so I don't laugh. But some comedy
is funny even when I don't understand the language. You know, like
people falling down and throwing pies and silly things like that.

LISTENING 1: Jackie Chan—Action-Comedy Hero
Listen for Main Ideas Page 106

Host: Welcome to our show. Today we introduce actor and **comedian**
Jackie Chan. We're going to talk about Jackie Chan's life and career,
and about what makes him so funny. The number is 877-555-1167.
Call us and tell us why you love Jackie Chan.

Now for a bit of background about Jackie. He's an international star of
many Hollywood movies. His fans know him for his exciting acting
style—his **powerful** jumps and kicks—and also his great **sense of humor**.

Chan was born in Hong Kong on April 7, 1954. In fact, his real name,
Chan Kong-Sang, means "born in Hong Kong." When he was very
young, he knew he wanted to be an actor. During his school days,
he studied at the China Drama Academy. He worked hard at school,
practicing Kung Fu and acting.

Jackie Chan's **professional** acting career began in Hong Kong in the mid-
1970s. His first movies were not popular. **However**, Chan didn't give up.
In 1978, he made several **hits** and became a big star in Hong Kong.

In the 1980s, Chan was ready to start his international career. So he
moved to Hollywood. But his first Hollywood **films** were not popular
in the U.S. And after a few years, he returned to Hong Kong. So how
did Chan become an international star?

Finally, in 1998, Hollywood director Brett Ratner asked Jackie to star
in the movie *Rush Hour*. This time, Americans loved the movie, and
they loved Jackie Chan. He became popular in the U.S., and today he is
still a **huge** international star.

So, what do you think makes Jackie Chan so funny? Let's go to the
phones and find out! Hello, you're on the air!

Fan 1: Hi. Uh,… This is Karen.

Host: Hi, Karen. Tell us why you love Jackie Chan.

Fan 1: Well, when I watch his movies, he just makes me laugh. I think it's because he smiles and laughs so much. I want to laugh, too. And he's also funny because he's so fast. I love watching his fight scenes. He's amazing.

Host: Yes, he is. Thanks, Karen. OK. Next caller, you're on the air.

Fan 2: Oh, um, hello. My name is Ernesto.

Host: Hi, Ernesto. Why do you think Jackie Chan is funny?

Fan 2: Well, I like his movies, but what I *love* about Jackie is his real personality—I mean, when he's <u>not</u> acting. When you watch him on TV, in an interview, he always tells very funny stories—stories about his life, about making movies… He's got a great sense of humor.

Host: That's great. Thank you for your call. All right. It looks like we have time for one more caller…. Next caller, what do you think….

Listen for Details Page 106

(Repeat Main Ideas track)

LISTENING SKILL: Listening for specific information
A. Page 107

(Repeat Main Ideas track)

B. Page 108

Host: Chan made two more *Rush Hour* movies, in 2001 and 2005. He also starred with actor Owen Wilson in the comedy movies, *Shanghai Noon* and *Shanghai Knights*. There are plans for a third *Shanghai* movie sometime in the future, called *Shanghai Dawn*.

In 2009, Chan starred in the Hong Kong drama The *Shinjuku Incident*. In this movie, Chan plays a more serious character—a Chinese worker who lives in Tokyo, Japan.

Does this serious role mean that Chan is giving up comedy? His fans hope not. They think comedy is what Jackie does best.

So long for now, listeners. Tune in next week when we'll….

LISTENING 2: Can Anyone Be Funny?
Listen for Main Ideas Page 110

Host: Thank you. Thank you. We have a great show for you today. Our guest is Mr. Larry Tate, the owner of the Comedy Center Theater. Welcome, Larry.

Larry: Thanks. It's great to be here.

Host: Larry, a lot of famous comedians started at your theater. What do you think makes a great comedian?

Larry: Well, Tina, I think anybody can be funny. The important thing is to try to find the humor in everyday life—the experiences that everyone can **understand**… like funny stories about our families, friends, or situations like going to the doctor.

Host: What other advice do you have for people who want to be funnier?

Larry: First of all, don't be shy about telling your funny stories. If you think they're funny, other people **probably** do, too. Here's one I like to tell. It's a true story about my three-year-old son:

One day at home, my son is very upset about something. I ask him why he's crying, and he tells me, "My new shoes hurt!" I look down at his shoes, and I say, "That's because you have them on the **wrong** feet." My son looks at me and says, "But these are the only feet I have."

Host: That's really funny. Kids really are some of the best comedians. Do you have any other tips?

Larry: Well, another tip I give new comedians is to **make fun of** yourself. It helps people feel relaxed. Here's a joke I often use:

One day, I'm at home. I turn on the TV and sit down on the sofa. My wife asks, "What are you doing?" I say, "Nothing." She says, "You did that yesterday." So I answer, "Yeah, I know. I wasn't finished."

Of course that story didn't really happen, but I use that joke as a funny way to connect with people.

Host: You're really good at this. OK. We have time for one more piece of advice.

Larry: OK. I guess one more tip I have is don't be **afraid** to show your **feelings**. A comedian is an actor. You need to **make eye contact** with the audience, and use your voice, your face, and your body to tell the story. It helps people **imagine** the story, and that makes it funnier.

Host: Great. Thanks a lot for being on the show, Larry. Join us next time when we….

Listen for Details Page 110

(Repeat Main Ideas track)

GRAMMAR: Simple present for informal narratives
A. Page 113

1. **Man:** A man and a woman go to a restaurant for lunch. The woman orders a bowl of soup. A few minutes later, the waiter brings the soup to the table. The man says, "Excuse me. Your finger's in my wife's soup." The waiter replies, "Oh, that's OK. It isn't too hot."

2. **Woman:** A woman's at the doctor's office. The doctor asks her, "What's the trouble?" The woman answers, "I hurt everywhere. It hurts when I touch my head. It hurts when I touch my leg, and it hurts when I touch my arm." The doctor thinks for a moment. Then he says "I know what's wrong… Your finger is broken!"

3. **Man:** A man stops his car at a traffic light. A policeman stops next to him and sees a penguin in the car. The policeman tells the man, "You can't drive with a penguin in your car. Take that penguin to the zoo." The man says, "Yes, sir. I will." The next day, the policeman sees the man's car again. The penguin is still in the car. The policeman asks, "Why do you have that penguin? I told you to take it to the zoo!" The man looks at the policeman and says, "I did that, and we had a great time! Today we're going to the movies!"

PRONUNCIATION: Simple present third-person -s and -es
Page 115

say	says	stop	stops
tell	tells	eat	eats
give	gives	change	changes
answer	answers	miss	misses
laugh	laughs	wash	washes
look	looks	watch	watches

SPEAKING SKILL: Using eye contact, pause, and tone of voice
Page 117

Speaker:… The man touches the rabbit, and the rabbit bites him. "Ouch!" He says, "You said your rabbit doesn't bite!" The shopkeeper replies, "That isn't my rabbit!"

Man: One day, I'm at home. I turn on the TV and sit down on the sofa. My wife asks, "What are you doing?" I say, "Nothing." She says, "You did that yesterday." So I answer, "Yeah, I know. I wasn't finished."

Woman: A woman's at the doctor's office. The doctor asks her, "What's the trouble?" The woman answers, "I hurt everywhere. It hurts when I touch my head. It hurts when I touch my leg, and it hurts when I touch my arm." The doctor thinks for a moment. Then he says, "I know what's wrong… Your finger is broken!"

UNIT ASSIGNMENT: Consider the Ideas
1. Page 118

Comedian (John): A tourist visits Sydney, Australia. He wants to go to the beach. But he doesn't know how to get there. He sees a policeman. He waves to the policeman and says, "Excuse me! Can you help me?" The policeman comes over and says, "Yes, sir. How can I help you?" The tourist says, "Can you tell me the fastest way to get to the beach?" The policeman asks, "Are you walking or driving?" The tourist answers, "Driving."

The policeman answers, "Well, that's the fastest way."

2. Page 119

(Repeat Consider the Ideas)

Unit 7: Music

The Q Classroom   Page 123

Teacher: Unit 7's Question is, "Why is music important to you?" Do you listen to music a lot, Yuna?

Yuna: Yes, I do.

Teacher: What kind?

Yuna: Mostly pop music.

Teacher: What do you like about that kind of music?

Yuna: It's fun. It makes me happy. I like to dance.

Teacher: How about you, Sophy? Is music important to you?

Sophy: Oh, yes. I listen to music when I work and when I exercise. It helps me get in the right mood. Some music relaxes me. Other music makes me energetic.

Teacher: Yes, music can change our mood, can't it? Why is music important to you, Marcus?

Marcus: Well, for me, music is an important part of my family life. We sing together a lot.

Teacher: What do you think Felix? Is music important to you?

Felix: Yes, very important. I play the guitar, and I express myself with music. I can say things with music that I can't say with words.

Preview the Unit
C. Page 124

[Brief excerpts from the following genres of music: Classical, Rock, Jazz, Pop]

LISTENING 1: Mind, Body, and Music
Listen for Main Ideas   Page 126

Professor: All right. Let's get started. For today's class, I've invited a special guest speaker. This is Dr. Tom Wilkins from the Music Science Center. Dr. Wilkins led a recent study on music and the **brain**, and he's going to tell us about that today. Please welcome him.

Dr. Wilkins: Good morning. Thank you for having me. Let's think for a moment about music in our lives. Music has always been a part of people's lives. We don't have any records of the first music, but scientists have found very, very old **instruments** such as drums and flutes made of animal skins and bones. Every culture in the world has music. It's part of what makes different cultures unique. Today I'm going to talk about some of the **benefits** of listening to music.

The first important benefit of music is that it can help us learn. For example, listening to classical music when we study activates both the left and the right sides of the brain. This makes our brain waves flow more freely. So the brain is **active** and ready to learn. We can **concentrate** and learn better. Studies show that children who learn to play musical instruments do better in school.

Another way that music is helpful is that it **improves** memory. Music activates the areas deep inside where the brain stores memories. Doctors can use music to help patients with brain diseases. Our research found that hearing familiar music can help people remember events and details from the past.

In addition, music can help people with physical problems, for example, older people, or those injured in an accident. When we **humans** hear music, we want to move. It's a natural physical response. Music can help older people stay active. One more important thing that music does is **lower stress**. Some types of music, such as classical music, cause the heart to slow down. And they cause the brain to make chemicals that relax us. Most people have stress from time to time. A lot of stress can cause health problems. So, listening to music has benefits for all of us…

Listen for Details   Page 126

(Repeat Main Ideas track)

LISTENING SKILL: Signal words and phrases
A. Page 128

1. The first important benefit of music is that it can help us learn. Listening to music makes the brain active, so we can concentrate and learn better.

2. In addition, music improves memory. Research shows that music can help people remember events and details from the past.

3. Another point is that music can help people with physical problems and can help older people stay active. It can also help people start to move again, even after many years of not moving.

4. Finally, music can help to lower stress. Some types of music, such as classical music, cause the heart rate to slow down. And they cause the brain to release chemicals that relax us.

LISTENING 2: Music in Our Lives
Listen for Main Ideas   Page 130

Maria: I listen to pop mostly. When I hear that **rhythm**, I have to get up and move… I have to dance. My friends and I have a dance group, and we get together and practice in the park sometimes. Listening to music brings my friends together. We're like a big family. When we hear a great new song, we share it with the rest of the group. Then we work on some dance moves together. Dancing helps me **express** who I am. It makes me feel like part of a **team**—I like that.

Jamal: I can't imagine my life without music. I play the guitar, and I write my own music—mostly rock or pop **tunes**. I don't play in a band or anything; I just enjoy playing by myself. Writing songs and playing my music lowers stress. My music gives me a way to **escape** from the rest of the world. When I'm making music, I can **forget** about my problems and my worries. Sometimes I feel like my guitar is my best friend.

Yoshiko: Singing is really popular in Japan. I like spending time with my friends at a "karaoke box." That's a place where you can get a **private** room and sing together. It's my favorite way to relax. I prefer singing Japanese pop songs, but they have all kinds of music. They even have **traditional** old Japanese songs, like the music my parents listen to. I think music is a really important part of my culture. I don't listen to traditional Japanese music very often, but I like it. It's special because people don't play that kind of music anywhere else. It's uniquely Japanese.

Alex: I play on a soccer team. Before every game, I enjoy taking a few minutes to myself—away from the rest of the team. I put on my headphones, and I listen to the same song by my favorite singer, Pitty. She's a rock musician from Brazil. Hearing her music really energizes me. After I hear it, I feel excited and ready to win. I definitely need music before every game.

Listen for Details Page 131

(Repeat Main Ideas track)

GRAMMAR: Gerunds as Subjects or Objects
A. Page 134

1. My friends and I have a dance group, and we get together and practice in the park sometimes. Listening to music brings my friends together. We're like a big family. When we hear a great new song, we share it with the rest of the group. Then we work on some dance moves together. Dancing helps me express who I am.

2. I just enjoy playing by myself. Writing songs and playing my music lowers stress. My music gives me a way to escape from the rest of the world. When I'm making music, I can forget about my problems and my worries.

3. Singing is really popular in Japan. I like spending time with my friends at a "karaoke box." That's a place where you can get a private room and sing together. It's my favorite way to relax. I prefer singing Japanese pop songs, but they have all kinds of music.

4. Before every game, I enjoy taking a few minutes to myself—away from the rest of the team. I put on my headphones, and I listen to the same song by my favorite singer, Pitty. She's a rock musician from Brazil. Hearing her music really energizes me.

PRONUNCIATION: Intonation in questions of choice
Page 135

Which do you like better, rock or pop?

Do you usually listen to new music or old music?

Do you prefer singing or dancing?

A. Page 136

1. Do you usually listen to music alone or with other people? [rising intonation over *alone*, falling over other *people*]

2. What's your favorite type of music? [falling intonation over *music*]

3. What is an example of traditional music from your country? [falling intonation over *country*]

4. Is your favorite singer from your country or another country? [rising intonation over *your country*, falling over *another country*]

5. When you study, do you listen to music, or do you prefer quiet? [rising intonation over *music*, falling intonation over *quiet*]

6. Do you enjoy singing in front of other people? [rising intonation over *other people*]

7. Which kind of music do you like better, classical or pop? [rising intonation over *rock*, falling over *pop*]

8. Do you prefer listening to music in English or in your own language? [rising intonation over *English*, falling intonation over *your own language*]

UNIT ASSIGNMENT: Consider the Ideas
Page 137

Steve: Hey Cem!

Cem: Hi Steve. How's it going?

Steve: Great. Thanks again for letting me interview you for my Music Studies class.

Cem: It sounds really interesting.

Steve: Yeah, it is. We have to interview students about their music preferences, so I'm just going to ask you a few questions about that.

Cem: OK.

Steve: OK, first, what kind of music do you like to listen to?

Cem: Well, I like a lot of different kinds of music, but my favorite is Turkish classical music.

Steve: Hmmm. Turkish classical music. Why do you like it?

Cem: Well, I feel calm and happy when I listen to it. It makes me think of home. I also think it's interesting that some European classical music of the 1700s uses a lot of Turkish instruments and sounds. Mozart's *Turkish Rondo* is really famous, for example.

Steve: Wow! Really? That is interesting. I don't think many people know that. So, who are your favorite musicians?

Cem: Well, let's see. Dede Efendi is probably the most famous Turkish classical music composer. I also like modern musicians, like Fazıl Say. He's a world-famous classical pianist and composer.

Steve: OK, great. Well, I think those are all of my questions for now. Thanks for your help.

Cem: You're welcome!

Unit 8: Honesty

The Q Classroom Page 141

Teacher: Today's Unit Question is "When is honesty important?" What do you think, Yuna? Is honesty important at school?

Yuna: Yes.

Teacher: How about at work?

Yuna: At work, yes.

Teacher: What about with your friends?

Yuna: Yes, very important.

Teacher: Honesty is important in all of those situations. Is honesty important all the time?

Felix: No, not always. It's important to be honest at school and work. But you don't want to be honest when it hurts someone—like telling your co-worker her dress is ugly.

Teacher: Yes, that's a little too honest. What do you think, Sophy? When is honesty important?

Sophy: I think honesty is important when dishonesty will have a bad result. For example, you can lie at work, and it can hurt the company. Or you can cheat at school and get in trouble.

Teacher: Good point. What about you, Marcus? When is honesty important?

Marcus: I agree with Sophy. And I also think that it's important to be honest with your friends. It's important for friends to trust each other.

LISTENING 1: Dishonesty in Schools
Listen for Main Ideas Page 144

Anchorwoman: What are young people learning in school these days? Not as much as they should, some experts say. Why?… Too many of them **cheat**—A recent **survey** in the U.S. found that about 75 percent of high school students cheat in school. They share test answers, look at classmates' test papers, and send text messages with answers during a test. And **according to** the survey, more than half of students also copy reports from the Internet. Our reporter, John Chi, talked to students and teachers about the problem of cheating at one school. Here's his report.

Reporter: Hi. I'm here at Oak Grove High School to talk to some of the teachers about the problem of cheating. Wendy Smith teaches history here. Wendy, what's going on? Are students just dishonest these days?

Wendy Smith: Well, John, I think it's all the new **technology** students have now. You know, they all have cell phones now, and they use the Internet for everything… Last year, about a **quarter** of my students turned in final reports that they copied from the Internet. Then this year, some of my students used cell phones to send text messages with test answers. I'd like to **prevent** students from using the Internet or sending text messages, but I think it's impossible.

Reporter: Hmm. I see. So, what did you do about it?

Wendy Smith: Well, I didn't want to believe it at first. I thought my students were truthful. All of the students received a zero for their work… Don't they know they are only hurting themselves by cheating?

Reporter: Thanks, Ms. Smith. We also have science teacher Don Quinn here with us. Mr. Quinn, do you feel the same way?

Don Quinn: Well, actually, I'm happy my students can use the Internet for research. It's really helpful and easy to use… but I guess it *can* create problems sometimes. Students shouldn't copy reports from websites. If they do that, they miss a chance to learn something interesting. I don't worry too much about cheating, though. I think my students are honest. They know that cheating is wrong, and they know I don't allow it.

Reporter: So, what can schools do about cheating? Can they stop it?

Don Quinn: Hmm. I'm not sure. I read an article about what schools in other countries are doing. The article said that in one African country, the government canceled about 25 percent of test scores after students cheated on tests. The article also said that some universities in China stop wireless phone messages, so students can't send text messages at school. And a university in Europe did a survey on cheating. According to the survey, a third of students answered that they cheated. So the university put cameras in all of its classrooms. I don't think we need to do anything like that at our school. It's a waste of time and money.

Reporter: Ms. Smith, do you agree with Mr. Quinn?

Wendy Smith: Actually, I think cameras in classrooms are a good idea. We need to do *something* here, Don. Students need to learn that school isn't just about **grades**. They need to study and work hard. If they cheat, they're the ones who are going to **suffer**.

Reporter: Well, thank you both very much. Join us next week for our program when we'll hear from some students about why they cheat, and whether they think cheating is wrong. You may be surprised by their answers!

Listen for Details Page 144
(Repeat Main Ideas track)

LISTENING SKILL: Making Inferences
A. Page 145

1. **Wendy Smith:** Well, John, I think it's all the new technology students have now. You know, they all have cell phones now, and they use the Internet for everything… Last year, about a quarter of my students turned in final reports that they copied from the Internet. Then this year, some of my students used cell phones to send text messages with test answers. I'd like to prevent students from using the Internet or sending text messages, but I think it's impossible.

2. **Reporter:** Hmm. I see. So, what did you do about it?

   Wendy Smith: Well, I didn't want to believe it at first. I thought my students were truthful. All of the students received a zero for their work… Don't they know they are only hurting themselves by cheating?

3. **Don Quinn:** Well, actually, I'm happy my students can use the Internet for research. It's really helpful and easy to use… but I guess it *can* create problems sometimes. Students shouldn't copy reports from websites. If they do that, they miss a chance to learn something interesting. I don't worry too much about cheating, though. I think my students are honest. They know that cheating is wrong, and they know I don't allow it.

4. **Don Quinn:**… The article also said that some universities in China stop wireless phone messages, so students can't send text messages at school. And a university in Europe did a survey on cheating. According to the survey, a third of students answered that they cheated. So the university put cameras in all of its classrooms. I don't think we need to do anything like that at our school. It's a waste of time and money.

5. **Reporter:** Ms. Smith, do you agree with Mr. Quinn?

   Wendy Smith: Actually, I think cameras in classrooms are a good idea. We need to do *something* here, Don. Students need to learn that school isn't just about grades.

LISTENING 2: What's the Right Thing to Do?
Listen for Main Ideas Page 147

1. **Daniela:** Hi, André. What are you working on?

   André: Oh, hi, Daniela. I'm just finishing my report for our culture class.

   Daniela: Finishing?! That was fast. I still have *a lot* of writing to do.

   André: Well, I'm writing about English education in different countries. I found a great website with some articles about that topic, and I just used **a little bit** from each article for my paper.

   Daniela: You mean… you copied your report directly from the Web?

André: No… I mean… not really. I didn't copy a whole article or anything. I just took small **sections** from several articles I found online and put them together. That's OK, isn't it?

Daniela: Hmm. Well, it's called plagiarism—

André: *Plagiar what?*

Daniela: Plagiarism—copying another person's writing and saying it's your own.

2. **Stephen:** Well, I think my resume is almost finished. I just need to add a few more things here under *Experience*… you know… to help me get the job at Braxton Books.

Chantal: Great. Can I see what you have **so far**?

Stephen: Sure. Here you go. Tell me what you think.

Chantal: Uh… Stephen. I think there's a mistake here. It says you were a manager at Horizon Restaurant, but you weren't a manager, you were a server, weren't you?

Stephen: Well, yes, I was a server, but I had *a lot* of **responsibility**. So I was *kind of* like a manager. It's not really a **lie**. Besides, this job at Braxton Books is for a manager. I'll never get the job if I don't have any experience as a manager.

3. **Liza:** Did you read that story in yesterday's paper, Drew? The one about the woman who **downloaded** music from the Internet?

Drew: No, I didn't see that one.

Liza: Well, according to the article, the woman downloaded 24 songs from an **illegal** music-sharing website.

Drew: Yeah. I think a lot of people do that. Did she **get caught**?

Liza: Yeah, she got caught, and she had to pay 80,000 dollars for *each song*. She had to pay almost *two million* dollars total!

Drew: Wow! Really? That's crazy. I mean, I don't understand why downloading music without paying for it is such a bad thing.

Listen for Details Page 148

(Repeat Main Ideas track)

VOCABULARY SKILL: Percentages and fractions
Page 150

1. A recent survey in the U.S. found that about 75 percent of high school students cheat in school. They share test answers, look at classmates' test papers, and send text messages with answers during a test. And according to the survey, more than half of students also copy reports from the Internet.

2. Last year, about a quarter of my students turned in final reports that they copied from the Internet.

3. I read an article about what schools in other countries are doing. The article said that in one African country, the government canceled about 25 percent of test scores after students cheated on tests.

4. And a university in Europe did a survey on cheating. According to the survey, a third of students answered that they cheated. So the university put cameras in all of its classrooms.

PRONUNCIATION: Linking consonants to vowels
Page 152

becau<u>se of</u>	a thir<u>d of</u>
qui<u>z a</u>nswers	no<u>t a</u>cceptable
fal<u>se i</u>nformation	ha<u>ve a</u> <u>lot of</u>

A. Page 153

1. I thin<u>k a</u> <u>lot of</u> people lie about thei<u>r a</u>ge.

2. I<u>s it</u> OK to keep money that you find in the street?

3. Abou<u>t a</u> quarte<u>r of</u> the student<u>s in</u> the class cheate<u>d on</u> the test.

4. Do you think it's OK to cal<u>l in</u> sick to work if you're not sick?

5. Becau<u>se of</u> the Internet, musician<u>s an</u>d bands don't ma<u>ke as</u> much money.

6. I<u>n our</u> English class, it's not OK to use a<u>n a</u>rticle from the Internet without giving credit.

SPEAKING SKILL: Sourcing information
A. Page 154

1. More than half of people take paper or pens from their company to use at home.

2. Over ten percent of people sometimes change the price tag to a lower price for something they want to buy.

3. About 20% of people give false information on a resume.

4. About 60% of people call in sick to work when they aren't sick.

5. Three quarters of people sometimes lie to friends or family to avoid hurting their feelings.

UNIT ASSIGNMENT: Consider the Ideas
A. Page 155

Nasir: First, I asked students how important honesty is, and 62 percent answered very important. The survey showed that 36 percent think it's a little important, and two percent of students think that honesty is not important. I was surprised about those results. I thought almost everyone thinks honesty is very important.

According to my survey, only about 25 percent of students are honest all the time. So that means that 75 percent—three quarters—of students are dishonest sometimes.

I also asked students how wrong they think some actions are. For example, I asked about not returning a library book, and ten percent answered "not wrong." Sixty-one percent said it was a little wrong, and 29 percent said it was very wrong.

The survey also found that 97 percent of students think hitting a car in a parking lot and not telling the owner is very wrong.

I also asked about cheating on a test. Nine percent answered "not wrong," but 66 percent—that's two thirds of students—think cheating on a test is very wrong, and 25 percent think it's a little wrong.

The survey showed that…

Unit 9: Life Changes

The Q Classroom Page 159

Teacher: The Unit Question for Unit 9 is "Is it ever too late to change?" Yuna, think about you and your parents. Is it easier for you to change or for your parents to change?

Yuna: Me. My parents don't like change.

Teacher: Do you think that's true? Do older people have a harder time with change?

Sophy: I think so. When you're young, everything is new and exciting. There are a lot of new and different things to try. When you're older, you like things to be the same. It's easier.

Teacher: So is it ever too late to change? Marcus?

Marcus: I don't think so. I think it depends on the person. Some people just like change. They like new experiences. I want to have lots of new experiences my whole life. I think it makes life more interesting.

Teacher: What do you think, Felix? When Marcus is older, will he discover that it's too late to change?

Felix: No, I agree with Marcus. I think change is harder for older people, but it's still possible. A few years ago, my parents moved to a new country. They got new jobs and learned a new language. That was a big change. But they have a positive attitude about change.

LISTENING 1: Attitudes about Change
Listen for Main Ideas Page 162

Professor: OK, everyone. Let's talk about last night's reading assignment. For homework, you read the list of English **proverbs** about change. What did you think about the proverbs, Andrea?

Andrea: I thought they were interesting, **especially**, "You can't teach an old dog new tricks." That was my favorite one. It means that when we get older, it's more difficult to change. Older people don't want to change their thinking or their lifestyle. They like things to stay the same.

Ali: Yes. We have a similar proverb in Morocco. We say, "An old cat will not learn how to dance."

Professor: Hmm. That's interesting… Yes, Franco, what do you think?

Franco: I don't know about that. I think older people *can* change. Everyone can change. It's important to be **flexible** at any age. I like the proverb that says, "It's never too late to change." I think that's a good attitude. The world is always changing. People need to change, too. In Brazil we say, "One who does not look ahead, **remains** behind." This means it's important to **accept** new ideas. You should always be ready to change.

Professor: …And what do you think, Juan Carlos?

Juan Carlos: I totally agree. In Spain, we say, "A wise man **changes his mind**, but a fool never will." It's always good to make a change. Like the proverb from the homework says, "All change is **progress**."

Professor: Katrina?

Katrina: Hmm. I'm not sure I agree. Change isn't *always* good. In Germany, we say, "To change and to improve are two different things." We should be careful when we change things. First, we should be sure the change will make things better.

Franco: That's true. The important thing is that we *can* change—I mean improve—if we want to. I like the proverb, "Life is what you make it." I think a lot of people are afraid to make changes. For example, last year, I was afraid to come to the U.S. to study. I never spent time in another country before, so it was a really big change for me. I thought it was easier to just stay in Brazil. But I knew I would miss a good **opportunity**. So, I just did it. I'm really happy I decided to come.

Andréa: Yes. It was difficult for me too at first. It was hard to be far away from my family. But I know I have to try new things if I want to change for the better.

Ali: Yes, you're right. Coming here from Morocco to study was a big change for me, too. But it was a good change. If we want to improve ourselves and our lives, we can't be afraid to take the first step.

Katrina: Yeah—It's great. We came to a new country and a new school, we made new friends, and we made a lot of progress with our

English… That's definitely a change for the better!… [Laughter from others] [fade out]

Listen for Details
Page 163

(Repeat Main Ideas track)

LISTENING SKILL: Listening for Different Opinions
A. Page 164

1. **Andrea:** It means that when we get older, it's more difficult to change. Older people don't want to change their thinking or their lifestyle. They like things to stay the same.

   Franco: I don't know about that. I think older people can change. Everyone can change. It's important to be flexible at any age.

2. **Franco:** In Brazil we say, "One who does not look ahead, remains behind." This means it's important to accept new ideas. You should always be ready to change.

   Juan Carlos: I totally agree. In Spain, we say, "A wise man changes his mind, but a fool never will."

3. **Juan Carlos:** It's always good to make a change. Like the proverb from the homework says, "All change is progress."

   Katrina: Hmm. I'm not sure I agree. Change isn't *always* good.

4. **Katrina:** We should be careful when we change things. First, we should be sure the change will make things better.

   Franco: That's true. The important thing is that we *can* change— I mean improve—if we want to.

LISTENING 2: Tips from a Life Coach
Listen for Main Ideas Page 167

Host: Welcome to our program today. We all have things we'd like to change about ourselves and our lives. Perhaps we want to be better students, exercise more, or start a new career. But how do we make these changes? And why are some **habits** so difficult to change? Professional life coach Diana Carroll is here with us today. And she'll take your phone calls and answer your questions later in the show. But first, let's meet her… Good afternoon, Diana.

Diana: Hi. Thank you for having me on your show.

Host: Diana, you're a "life coach." What does that mean?

Diana: Well, Ted, a life coach is someone who helps people make changes to improve their lives. Many people want to change their lives, but they aren't sure how to get started. Or maybe they are *able* to make a change, but they can't **stick to** it. They go back to their old habits after a short time. I give **advice** to people who want to make changes in their lives.

Host: I see. And what *kinds* of changes do you help your people with?

Diana: I help people with all kinds of changes—big and small. Some people want to make really big changes in their lives, for example, to find a new job or career, or to move to a new city. Others want to break bad habits such as overeating or watching too much TV. And others want to change something about their personalities, for example, they want to be more friendly or flexible.

Host: All right. Well, let's take our first caller now. Caller? Are you there?

Caller: Yes, uh… hi, Diana.

Diana: Hello, there. What's your question?

Caller: Well, I really want to change my lifestyle. My job is really busy. I work too much, and I don't have much time to eat well or exercise. I'd like to be healthier. What do you **recommend**?

Diana: Good question. A lot of people want to be healthier…Here's my advice: The first step is to set small **goals** for yourself. Many people try to make too many big changes quickly. If you set small goals, you have a better chance of success. Let's start with exercise. Do you have any free time in your day when you could get a little exercise?

Caller: Hmm. Well, I do have a little time during my lunch break.

Diana: Great. How about taking a short walk two or three days a week?

Caller: Yeah… I think I could do that.

Diana: You see? That's a small goal that you can do. OK, my next piece of advice is to write down your goal.

Caller: Write down my goal?

Diana: Yes. Studies show that people who write down their goals **achieve** them more often. Be sure to put the piece of paper with your goal someplace where you'll see it often—on the refrigerator, or on the wall above your desk. This will **remind** you of your goal every time you see it.

Caller: OK. I'm writing it right now!…. Exercise… walk… three days a week… There.

Diana: It really works. OK, are you ready for the next step?

Caller: Yes!

Diana: You need to share your goal with someone—for example, a co-worker or a friend… someone who can help you achieve your goal.

Caller: You mean, I should tell someone about it?

Diana: Yes. That's right. That person can **encourage** you and help you stick to your plan.

Caller: OK. I'll do it.

Diana: All right. The next thing I tell people is to set a date to complete the goal.

Write the date when you plan to **achieve** your goal. Be prepared to change your goals, or to give yourself more time.

Caller: Uh huh… set a date to complete goal.

Diana: Yes. Then you need to check your progress every week. So, for example, at the end of every week, you can write down how much you exercised that week. Keep it in a notebook.

Caller: OK. I can do that.

Diana: And here's the final bit of advice: when you reach your goal, be sure to celebrate your success. Buy yourself a gift… Go out to dinner at your favorite restaurant… Remember that it's hard work to make a change. As I tell people, don't be afraid to make changes. Change isn't always easy. You may not succeed the first time, but you can do anything if you're willing to keep trying.

Caller: Thank you so much. You really helped me today. I'm definitely going to follow your advice.

Host: Yes. Well, thanks for calling in. Let's take one more call now…

Listen for Details Page 167

(Repeat Main Ideas track)

VOCABULARY SKILL: Verb + noun collocations
A. Page 169

1. Some people want to make really big changes in their lives, for example, to find a new job or career, or to move to a new city.

Others want to break bad habits, such as overeating or watching too much TV. And others want to change something about their personalities—for example, they want to become more friendly or more flexible.

2. You need to share your goal with someone—for example, a co-worker or a friend… someone who can help you achieve your goal.

3. I give advice to people who want to make changes in their lives.

4. In Spain, we say, "A wise man changes his mind, but a fool never will."

5. Many people want to change their lives, but they aren't sure how to get started. Or maybe they are able to make a change, but they can't stick to it.

6. And we made a lot of progress with our English… That's definitely a change for the better!

7. Thank you so much. You really helped me today. I'm definitely going to follow your advice.

8. The first step is to set small goals for yourself. Many people try to make too many big changes quickly.

PRONUNCIATION: Content word stress in sentences
Page 172

1. **Life** is what you **make** of it.

2. Be the **change** you **want** to see in the **world**.

3. It's **never** too **late** to **change**.

4. To **change** and to **improve** are two **different things**.

A. Page 173

1. To **learn** is to **change**.

2. A **change** is as **good** as a **rest**.

3. **Change** your **thoughts**, and you **change** your **world**.

4. To **improve** is to **change**; to be **perfect** is to **change often**.

5. When the **music changes**, so does the **dance**.

6. You **change** your **life** by **changing** your **heart**.

B. Page 173

[Repeat sentences in Exercise A.]

UNIT ASSIGNMENT: Consider the ideas
Page 174

Mei Ling: I'm going to explain how to break the habit of watching too much TV. First, you need to make a TV schedule. For one week, write down, every day, all the times you watch TV. Be sure to write down the time you start and the time you stop. Does that make sense?

Group of students: Yeah/Uh-huh/Yes

Mei Ling: Then you need to set a goal for watching less. Try to watch TV only half the time you usually do. For example, if you usually watch ten hours a week, set a goal of watching five hours a week. OK…? Next, make a list of other activities you like to do in your free time, besides watching TV. Be sure to choose things you enjoy. For example, reading, jogging, or spending time with friends. Are there any questions?

Student 1: Yes, um. How many activities should I write?

Mei Ling: Oh, I think three or four is enough. Then after you make your list, look at your TV schedule. Choose one or two hours when you usually watch TV, and write down one of the activities on your list instead. For the first week, just do one other activity instead of watching TV. Be careful not to start too fast. Is that clear?

Group of students: Yeah/Uh-huh/Yes

Mei Ling: Every week, add one more activity into your schedule, and you'll see that you're not watching TV so much, and you are doing many other things that you enjoy… Finally, celebrate when you achieve your goal—have a party, go out to dinner—you worked hard! Good job!

Unit 10: Fear

The Q Classroom Page 179

Teacher: The Unit Question for Unit 10 is "When is it good to be afraid?" So when are you afraid? Yuna?

Yuna: I'm afraid of spiders and I'm afraid on airplanes.

Teacher: Are those good fears?

Yuna: No.

Teacher: Why not? Marcus, do you think it's good for Yuna to be afraid of spiders and airplanes?

Marcus: Well, spiders and airplanes aren't usually dangerous. Most spiders don't hurt people and most airplanes don't crash. Those fears can make you unhappy for no reason.

Teacher: Good point. Is it ever good to be afraid? Felix?

Felix: Well, it's good to be afraid of things that can actually hurt you—like dangerous sports, for example. It can make you more careful.

Teacher: What do you think, Sophy? When is it good to be afraid?

Sophy: I agree with Felix. It's good to be afraid of things that can hurt you. Our fear keeps us safe. But sometimes we're afraid even when we aren't really in danger. Like Yuna knows that most spiders can't hurt her. But some can, and that's why she is afraid of them.

LISTENING 1: The Science of Fear
Listen for Main Ideas Page 182

Presenter: Welcome, ladies and gentlemen. Thank you for coming today. The title of my presentation is "The Science of Fear." First, I'm going to discuss some of the different types of fear. Then I'll talk about the physical effects of fear—that is, what happens in our bodies when we feel fear. And finally, I'll go over the **purposes** of fear—why we feel fear and what it does for us.

Alright. Let's first start with the question, what is fear? Fear is an emotion, like happiness, sadness, or love. We, humans, feel fear when we believe that we are in some kind of danger. The situations that make us feel fear may be different depending on the person. For example, one person may be afraid of flying in an airplane, and so feels fear when he or she travels. However, another person may have no fear at all of flying. Different people are afraid of different things.

There are also several different types of fear. For example, **anxiety**—or worry—is a common type of fear. This is when we feel fear about something that may happen in the future. The most common anxieties are about money, work, and personal relationships. Panic is another type of fear. Panic is a sudden, strong feeling of fear. When we **panic**, the fear takes over our body and mind, and we can't think clearly. Another kind of fear is a **phobia**. A phobia is a very strong fear of a particular person, place, or thing. For example, people may have a phobia of animals, such as snakes or spiders, or they may be afraid of a situation, such as being in a high place or being closed in a small space. Sometimes people can **get over** their phobias with the help of a doctor.

One thing that's important to remember, though, is that fear isn't always a bad feeling… some people actually enjoy feeling fear, like people who enjoy horror movies. They feel excited by fear, and it gives them a kind of energy.

OK. Does that make sense? Can I move on to the effects of fear?

Audience: Yes, Uh huh, Yeah

Alright. You probably know what you feel like when you feel afraid. But what's really going on inside your body? When you first feel fear, your brain quickly makes chemicals that cause different physical reactions. First, your body gets warmer and you begin to **sweat**. Soon after that, you may be able to hear your heart beating in your ears, and you may even feel it in your chest. This is because your heart beats much faster than usual. Your body becomes strong and tight all over. You may even be able to do amazing things. For example, you may suddenly see, smell, or hear very well, or you may have the **strength** to lift something very, very heavy. There are many stories of people who lifted cars or other heavy objects to save a person who was underneath them.

Audience: Wow! Hmm. Interesting

Now, let's discuss the purpose of fear. Why do we feel fear, and what does it do for us? We know that we usually feel fear when there is some kind of danger. When our bodies react to fear, we suddenly have energy and strength to fight—or, if we choose, to run away from the danger. So, we can say that the basic purpose of fear is to **protect** us from danger.

OK. Is that clear? Are there any questions?

Audience member: Yes. I have a question. You talked about horror movies. What are some other examples of…

Listen for Details Page 182

(Repeat Main Ideas track)

LISTENING SKILL: Taking Classification Notes
A. Page 184

Presenter: OK. Does that make sense? Can I move on to the effects of fear?

Audience: Yes, Uh huh, Yeah

Presenter: Alright. You probably know what you feel like when you feel afraid. But what's really going on inside your body? When you first feel fear, your brain quickly makes chemicals that cause different physical reactions. First, your body gets warmer and you begin to sweat. Soon after that, you may be able to hear your heart beating in your ears, and you may even feel it in your chest. This is because your heart beats much faster than usual. Your body becomes strong and tight all over. You may even be able to do amazing things. For example, you may suddenly see, smell, or hear very well, or you may have the strength to lift something very, very heavy. There are many stories of people who lifted cars or other heavy objects to save a person who was underneath them.

B. Page 184

Presenter: OK. Is that clear? Are there any questions?

Audience member: Yes. I have a question. You talked about horror movies. What are some other examples of things people do because they want to feel fear?

Presenter: Well, let's see… Another common example is going on fast rides and roller coasters at theme parks like Disneyland. Many people love the feeling of moving very, very fast. It's scary, but it's also exciting and fun. Some people may drive very fast cars or motorcycles. There are also many sports that people actually enjoy *because* they are scary or dangerous—some examples of those are adventure sports such as skydiving and bungee jumping. Those are just a few examples. Does that answer your question?

Audience member: Yes, thank you. But I have one more question.

Presenter: Alright.

Audience member: Why do some people enjoy fear and others don't? My husband loves horror movies and roller coasters—but I hate them.

Presenter: That's a great question. Scientists found that the difference is in the brain. We know that fear is a response to real danger. But, when we watch a horror movie, for example, there is no real danger to us. It's just a movie. Some people's brains send a message that says, "Don't worry. There's no real danger." That way they feel the physical effects of fear—the excitement and the energy, but they know it isn't real, so they can enjoy the feeling. Other people's brains send a message that there *is* real fear, even when they watch a movie or ride a roller coaster. When our brain senses real fear, we feel stress, and we do not enjoy the feeling of fear.

LISTENING 2: What Are You Afraid of?
Listen for Main Ideas   Page 185

Receptionist: Marcie Davis—the doctor is ready to see you now.

Marcie: Oh, OK. Thank you.

Doctor: Hi, Marcie. Come on in. You can have a seat right here.

Marcie: Thank you, Doctor Travis.

Doctor: OK, let's see. This is your first visit… so… today I'd like to hear about what's **bothering** you, and we can begin to talk about ways to help you get over your phobia.

Marcie: OK. That sounds good.

Doctor: So…Can you describe the problem and tell me when it first started…? Go ahead. I'm all ears.

Marcie: All right. Um… let's see. Well, the problem is that I'm **terrified** of high places. It started when I was about 12 years old. I had this dream—a **nightmare**, actually. In the nightmare, I was on top of a tall building looking down over the city. There was no way down. I started to panic… I started falling so fast… I felt so terrified. When I woke up, I was sweating and shaking like a leaf. I still have that same nightmare… often. Sometimes I can't sleep at night.

Doctor: Uh huh. I see. And can you tell me about some of the situations that make you feel afraid?

Marcie: Well, I can't stand being up above the **ground**—even just a little bit. I can't do the things **normal** people do. I can't go hiking; I can't go inside tall buildings.

Doctor: Hmm. It sounds like this phobia—this strong fear of high places—has a very **negative** effect on your life.

Marcie: You can say that again. It really makes my life difficult. There are so many things I want to do, but I just can't… Last week a group of my friends went rock climbing. Of course they invited me, just to be nice, but they knew I wouldn't go. And a few months ago, I found a great job online. It was the **ideal** job for me. But the company was all the way on the other side of town. If I got the job, I'd have to drive across the Springfield Bridge every day! I can't cross a big bridge like that! So, I guess I'll just keep the job I have—even though my boss drives me crazy.

Doctor: Marcie, I can understand your feeling upset over this. This is a very common phobia, and people do get over it. It will take some time, but I think slowly you *can* learn to live a normal life.

Marcie: Really? Oh, I hope so. What do I need to do?

Doctor: Well, to get over a phobia, you have to stop avoiding the things that scare you. In your situation, you need to begin to see and visit high places. I'll help you with this… We'll start slowly. For example, we'll begin by looking at some photos of high places. You may have a hard time looking at the photos at first, but you will **get used to** it before you know it. Then when you're ready, we'll begin with some real experiences. We'll go upstairs to the second floor, and we'll just look out the window… Then we'll…

Listen for Details   Page 186

(Repeat Main Ideas track)

PRONUNCIATION: Linked vowel sounds with /w/ or /y/
A.   Page 190

Examples

you are [linking /w/ sound]

who is [linking /w/ sound]

go up [linking /w/ sound]

Examples

I am [linking /y/ sound]

she is [linking /y/ sound]

we aren't [linking /y/ sound]

B.   Page 191

1. Are you afraid of bats? [linking /w/ sound]

2. Why are you scared of snakes? [linking /y/ sound]

3. Julio is afraid of high places. [linking /w/ sound]

4. She always screams when she hears thunder. [linking /y/ sound]

5. Do you know anyone at this party? [linking /w/ sound]

6. She is making me nervous. [linking /y/ sound]

7. I don't see anyone I know here. [linking /y/ sound]

8. I know three other people who have a phobia of closed spaces. [linking /y/ sound]

UNIT ASSIGNMENT: Consider the Ideas
Page 193

A: Last summer, after I graduated from college, I took a camping trip to the Green Mountains. I went with two of my best friends, Julianne and Jake. We wanted to make sure we were not close to other hikers, so we hiked really far into the trees. It was so beautiful out there in the woods. Anyway, one night, we were sleeping, and we heard something outside our tent.

B: What was it?

A: It was a huge black bear!

B: No way! What did you do?

A: Well, I'm terrified of bears, so I panicked… I was shaking like a leaf! My friends Julianne and Jake knew I was scared, but they stayed calm. They tried to use their cell phones to call the emergency number, but their cell phones didn't work.

B: How awful. So, what happened?

A: Well, luckily, Jake had a radio. He turned the radio on and put the volume really high. The loud noise scared the bear away.